Accountants Without Standards?

*Compulsion or Evolution in
Company Accounting*

D.R. MYDDELTON

*Professor of Finance and Accounting,
Cranfield School of Management*

Published by
INSTITUTE OF ECONOMIC AFFAIRS
1995

First published in October 1995

by

THE INSTITUTE OF ECONOMIC AFFAIRS
2 Lord North Street, Westminster,
London SW1P 3LB

Hobart Paper 128

ISSN 0073-2818

ISBN 0-255 36372-9

Many IEA publications are translated into languages other
than English or are reprinted. Permission to translate or to
reprint should be sought from the Editorial Director at the
above address.

Cover design by David Lucas

Printed in Great Britain by
BOURNE PRESS LIMITED, BOURNEMOUTH, DORSET
Set in Baskerville Roman 11 on 12 point

CONTENTS

[4]

FOREWORD

Despite the Government's professed wish to deregulate, there is evidence of increasing regulation of activities, both commercial and personal. Restrictions on contractual arrangements, whether in the name of worker or consumer protection, safeguarding the environment, enhancing health and safety or for other reasons, are now common. New regulations are often responses to dramatic events or supposed crises: someone, it is thought, should be seen to be doing something.

But what of accounting? Is there not a clear-cut case for the imposition of standards to ensure that potential investors and others can obtain a 'true and fair view' of a company's affairs? In *Hobart Paper No. 128*, Professor David Myddelton – a distinguished academic accountant and one of the Institute's Managing Trustees – argues persuasively that the

> '. . . "authority" claimed for accounting standards, especially those dealing with measurement, is unwise in intellectual and commercial matters' (below, p.62).

Professor Myddelton begins (Section I) with a brief history of accounting standards, mainly in Britain, though he makes comparisons with the United States and other countries. As he points out, since 1990, under the Accounting Standards Board, Financial Reporting standards are '. . . in effect mandatory' (p.15). Another set of compulsory *de facto* accounting standards exists in the Companies Acts which have devoted more and more space to company accounts, sometimes duplicating and sometimes contradicting 'normal' accounting standards.

Section II of the *Hobart Paper* reviews the arguments for and against standards. Professor Myddelton argues that one effect of standards in accounting, as in other fields, may be to stop desirable evolution. Bad accounting may be legitimised and independent judgement may be stifled.

Section III discusses the purpose of company accounts, starting from the American FASB's conceptual framework project of the mid-1970s. In Myddelton's view, echoes of this project linger on, driven by academics who seek '. . . a comprehensive, self-consistent, "scientific" deductive system of accounting' (p.38).

But, he says, standard-setters should not forbid particular treatments of accounts: there should be '. . . freedom to differ where those responsible think it right' (p.39), though companies should disclose which treatment they use.

After discussing in Section IV the setting and enforcing of standards, and the problems which have arisen both in Britain and the United States from political interference in standard setting, Professor Myddelton turns (Section V) to an assessment of the case for and against compulsory standards.

He believes the arguments in favour of compulsion to be weak. Voluntary standards ('Suggestions') seem to him more appropriate, since they do not inhibit evolution and do not rule out methods which would provide a 'true and fair view'. Nevertheless, he recognises that Suggestions might not remain voluntary for long, because some 'representative body' might move in to co-ordinate them. A way forward might therefore be to accept that there will be standards, but to make them relate to adequate disclosure rather than detailed prescription of methods of measurement.

Professor Myddelton urges that the way should be left open for '. . . an independent profession to help accounting to evolve freely' (p.62). The emphasis should be on disclosure requirements for listed companies, though probably less than now:

'. . . accounting standards should be limited to disclosure requirements. They should not attempt to prescribe rules on measurement' (p.63).

In all IEA publications, the views expressed are those of the author, not of the Institute (which has no corporate view), its Trustees, Advisers or Directors. David Myddelton's paper is published to stimulate debate about how best to achieve 'true and fair' statements of a company's affairs.

October 1995   COLIN ROBINSON
Editorial Director, Institute of Economic Affairs;
Professor of Economics, University of Surrey

THE AUTHOR

D.R. MYDDELTON was educated at Eton and the Harvard Business School. He is a chartered accountant. Since 1972 he has been Professor of Finance and Accounting at the Cranfield School of Management. He is Chairman of the Academic Advisory Council of the University of Buckingham and a Managing Trustee of the Institute of Economic Affairs.

Professor Myddelton has written many books and articles. His textbooks include: *The Meaning of Company Accounts* (5th edn. 1992), with Professor Walter Reid; *Essential Management Accounting* (2nd edn. 1993), with M. W. Allen; and *The Essence of Financial Management* (1995). He has also written *On a Cloth Untrue: Inflation Accounting, the way forward* (1984) and *The Power to Destroy: a study of the British tax system* (2nd edn. 1994). He has contributed to IEA publications on the subjects of tax and inflation.

ACKNOWLEDGEMENTS

I am grateful to the following for commenting on an earlier draft and so helping me to improve this paper: Henry Gold, Professor John Grinyer, Roger Myddelton, Professor David Pendrill, Malcolm Raiser, Professor Peter Watson and two anonymous referees. I would also like to thank Professor Colin Robinson for his friendly support and Sheila Hart at Cranfield for her work on revising drafts and producing the final text.

D. R. M.

I. THE EMERGENCE OF ACCOUNTING STANDARDS

A True and Fair View

For nearly half a century British company law has required accounts to give 'a true and fair view' of the state of a company's affairs and of its profit or loss for the financial year. A true and fair view implies 'consistent application of generally accepted accounting principles'.[1] But *more than one* true and fair view is possible: the word 'a' is important. The 1879 Companies Act required 'a true and correct view' of the state of affairs: the change in 1947 to 'a true and fair view' may have come because some people felt that in dealing with estimates the word 'correct' was too rigid.[2]

The EEC Fourth Directive in 1974 adopted the British call for 'a true and fair view' as an overriding requirement for company accounts in all member-states. This was a great compliment to the high quality of British accounting, which accounting standards had then hardly affected. In the UK, as in the USA, capital market pressures had strongly influenced accounts. In the rest of Europe governments often dictated accounting rules to meet fiscal objectives, which produced lower quality accounting than in the UK. It is, however, clear that not all countries interpret the requirement for 'a true and fair view' in the same way.[3]

There have been few judicial rulings to help accountants and others understand what the British courts think 'a true and fair view' means. The Foreword to Accounting Standards claims that compliance with accounting standards will normally be essential for financial statements to give a true and fair view. And the

---

[1] Institute of Chartered Accountants in England and Wales (ICAEW), Recommendation N18, 1958.

[2] B.A. Rutherford, 'The True and Fair View Doctrine: A Search for Explication', *Journal of Business Finance and Accounting*, Winter 1985.

[3] David Alexander and Simon Archer, *The European Accounting Guide*, London: Academic Press, 1992, p.20.

Companies Act[4] now requires companies to say whether their accounts follow accounting standards and to give details, with reasons, if not.

Arden[5] suggests that courts are likely to find that, in order to show a true and fair view, accounts must normally comply with accounting standards. This would be so even if a standard were to require a treatment that is neither generally accepted nor prevails in practice. But her opinion that, in effect, accounting standards themselves almost amount to laws has not yet been directly tested. It implies that whether a set of accounts gives a true and fair view depends more on compliance with rules than on independent professional judgement. If that is so, two questions become critical: who sets the rules? and on what basis?

Recommendations, 1945-1969

From 1945 to 1969, the Institute of Chartered Accountants in England and Wales (ICAEW) produced for its members a series of Recommendations on Accounting Principles. They were voluntary guidelines to best practice, which often allowed for different approaches. The topics included: tax, inflation, group accounts, valuing stock, and the format of accounts.

In 1969 the ICAEW also began to publish *Financial Reporting: a survey of UK published accounts*. This annual series illustrates accounting treatments and shows the extent of various practices (often by sampling 300 companies of various sizes). The monthly 'Company Reporting' has fulfilled a similar function since 1990. Both are useful in showing which accounting practices seem to be common, and in exposing and commenting on problem areas.

Towards the end of this period, discontent with the accounting profession flared up when, in October 1967, GEC made a take-over bid for AEI. In response, the AEI directors forecast a pre-tax profit for the calendar year 1967 of £10 million. After GEC won control, the final AEI 1967 accounts disclosed a £4½ million *loss*. A subsequent inquiry ascribed about £5 million of the difference to matters of fact and £9½ million to matters of

---

4   The Companies Act 1985, Section 36A.

5   Mary Arden, 'Accounting Standards Board: The True and Fair Requirement', Appendix to the Foreword to *Accounting Standards*, London: Accounting Standards Board, 1993.

judgement. The latter was largely due to different views about the likely outcome of certain long-term contracts. (AEI group sales were £260 million a year, and stocks and work-in-progress about £100 million. One 1967 pound equals nearly 10 1995 pounds in terms of purchasing power.)

The ICAEW felt it had to respond to the GEC/AEI 'scandal'. Otherwise it was afraid that the *government* would interfere -which everyone took for granted would be the worst possible outcome. As a result, in December 1969 the ICAEW published a Statement of Intent 'to advance accounting standards' by:

- publishing authoritative statements on best accounting practice;

- exposing draft accounting standards more widely;

- recommending disclosure of accounting bases when accounts include significant items which depend on judgement or estimates;

- recommending disclosure of departures from accounting standards.

The accounting aspects of the GEC/AEI takeover were a storm in a teacup: they probably surprised only people who knew very little about accounting, or about commercial life. Indeed, the problems behind the AEI profit forecasts still exist today. According to Custis:

'At the ICAEW conference at Cambridge in June 1979, we considered the "spectacular mistakes" of the sixties which were among the influences leading to the introduction of accounting standards. The general opinion was that the problems of AEI-GEC, Pergamon, Vehicle and General, and so on, would not have been prevented by our existing accounting standards.'[6]

Department of Trade and Industry inspectors investigating another more recent scandal,[7] took a similar view. They did not believe that the absence of an accounting standard dealing with

---

[6] P.J. Custis, 'Reporting Corporate Performance - For What Purpose?' (Deloitte Lecture at Birmingham, October 1979), in *Contemporary Issues in Accounting*, Bath: Pitman Publishing, May 1984, p.21.

[7] *Report of DTI Inspectors on Atlantic Computers plc*, London: DTI, July 1994, para. 5.109.

lease broking was a material cause of the deficiencies in the accounts of Atlantic Computers plc between 1981 and 1988. (We cannot tell, of course, how many scandals accounting standards may have helped to prevent.)

The stimulus for *ad hoc* accounting regulation has often been so-called 'scandals', as governments are unwilling to be seen to tolerate them. But this is a political, not an economic, reason. The United States government set up the Securities and Exchange Commission following the Wall Street Crash of 1929. Yet there was little evidence to show that poor or misleading disclosure caused losses to investors.[8] A non-problem followed by a non-solution! Perhaps that sums up the history of accounting standards.

The Accounting Standards Committee, 1970-1990

At first the Accounting Standards Steering Committee was a committee of the ICAEW alone. (The 'Steering' was dropped after several years.) But the Scottish Institute was reluctant to be left out. Until then it had chosen not to issue guidelines to its own members, on the grounds that they might discourage future progress and embarrass members who disagreed with them. So in the end the Accounting Standards Committee contained up to 20 part-time unpaid delegates from all the main accounting bodies, each of which had to approve every standard.

Failure to comply with the ASC's statements of standard accounting practice (SSAPs) might cause the auditors to 'qualify' their report. Members of the profession were to try to observe standards, or, if not, to disclose and explain significant departures from them. (Accounting standards were not a comprehensive code of rigid rules.) In judging exceptional or borderline cases it would be important to have regard to the spirit of accounting standards and to bear in mind the overriding requirement to give a true and fair view.

The ASC issued 18 standards (SSAPs) in its first decade, seven in its second (see Appendix 1, below, p.65). The later standards tended to deal with difficult topics, more to do with measurement than disclosure, often requiring a longer gestation period. Many standards were revised at least once. Towards the end of its life

---

[8]   George J. Benston, *Corporate financial disclosure in the UK and the USA*, Farnborough, Hants.: Saxon House, 1976, p.19.

the ASC also issued a flurry of exposure drafts, some of which later became standards, for example FRS 1 on cash flow statements. Others are still waiting, for example ED 47 on Goodwill.

The best-selling tome *UK GAAP*[9] pays a warm tribute to the former Accounting Standards Committee:

> 'In retrospect, its achievements were considerable, given the modest resources available to it, and although some of its standards can be criticised, collectively they improved UK GAAP beyond recognition from the state of financial reporting practice at the time of its creation in 1970.'

Post hoc ergo propter hoc. The quality of UK accounting would almost certainly have improved and developed even in the absence of accounting standards, as it did in the preceding 20 years. The proper contrast with 1990 is not the starting point in 1970 but what the 1990 position would have been without the ASC. There have indeed been some improvements since 1970: in disclosure of accounting policies, in valuing stocks, in capitalising finance leases. But there have been disasters too: in inflation accounting, in deferred tax, in accounting for goodwill.

During much of the ASC's life the difficult problem of inflation accounting was on the agenda. Government interference made things worse (see Section 4, 'Political Interference', below, p.54). On this topic, the ASC clearly failed and lost confidence. Equally important, others lost confidence in it. In particular there was concern about the ASC's 'lack of teeth' to enforce its standards. As a result, in November 1987, the Consultative Committee of Accountancy Bodies (CCAB) set up a Committee to review the standard-setting process. The Dearing Committee[10] acknowledged 'a small body of opinion' holding that standards inhibit preparers and auditors of accounts from applying their expert judgement and that, on balance, standards hinder rather than help the development of fair financial reporting.

But Dearing concluded that the balance of argument was strongly in favour of the 1970 decision to develop accounting standards. This was because of the complexity of the decisions

---

9   Mike Davies, Ron Paterson and Allister Wilson, *UK GAAP*, London: Macmillan for Ernst & Young, 4th edn. 1994, pp. 17-18.

10 ICAEW, *The Making of Accounting Standards* (Report of the Review Committee under the Chairmanship of Sir Ron Dearing), September 1988, pp. 7 and 18.

faced by the preparers and auditors of accounts; the pressures to which they can be exposed; the need to avoid ambiguity; and the value of having information prepared on a consistent, fair and reasonably comparable basis.

The Dearing Committee said the purpose of accounting standards was to provide authoritative but not mandatory guidance on the interpretation of what constitutes a true and fair view. This seems close to the aim of the ICAEW's Recommendations, dating back to 1945. The Committee went on:

> 'Our recommendations are concerned with increasing [sic] the quality and timeliness of accounting standards, reducing the permitted options, and promoting compliance with them.'

These led in 1990 to the formation of the Financial Reporting Council and the Accounting Standards Board.

The Accounting Standards Board, 1990 to the Present

> 'Enter the Accounting Standards Board. What is needed, so the story goes, is a group which will not knuckle under to the vested interests of client groups, which will not "fiddle while Rome burns" and one which will act decisively to restore to its once glorious heights the public's faith in financial reporting. A new group, untarnished by the problems of the past and better constituted to overcome its predecessor's shortcomings can give the public what it expects. Or can it?'

The above paragraph was written in 1973 about the United States.[11] It fits the UK well in 1990, when the ASB replaced the ASC. I have merely changed the (US) Financial Accounting Standards Board (FASB) to the (UK) Accounting Standards Board at the beginning.

The Accounting Standards Board differed from its forerunner, the Accounting Standards Committee, in a number of ways, largely as a result of Dearing's views. Two of the ASB's members are full-time: the chairman and a technical director. There are only nine or 10 members (compared with about 20 on the ASC); and there have already been several changes. ASB members are appointed by a Financial Reporting Council comprising about

---

[11] John Shank, 'The Pursuit of Accounting Standards - Whither and Whence', *Journal of Contemporary Business*, Spring 1973, p.86.

25 representatives of various parties concerned with company accounts - preparers, auditors, users.

Despite Dearing's statement of purpose, under the new system Financial Reporting Standards (FRSs) are in effect mandatory. The new régime's enforcement body, the Review Panel, aims not to punish offenders, but to ensure that companies produce accounts of adequate quality. It has so far considered about 45 cases a year. Of the 75 per cent that were pursued, slightly more than half required some corrective action, often publishing amended accounts in subsequent years.

Following the US example, there is also an Urgent Issues Task Force (UITF), to deal quickly with important emerging problems. The ASB may have up to three dissenters in issuing an accounting standard; but the UITF may have no more than two out of a maximum voting membership of 15 with respect to its 'abstracts'. These are not-quite-standards.

The ASB has issued seven Financial Reporting Standards in its first five years (see Appendix 1, below, pp.65-66, for details), three of them relating more to disclosure than to measurement. As usual there was a 'honeymoon period', which is now over. And as usual some of the trickiest outstanding problems have been left to stew for a while. With the ASC the most obvious was inflation accounting; with the ASB it is probably goodwill and intangible assets.

The ASB has dealt with a number of issues (cash flow statements, 'extraordinary' items, capital instruments, acquisitions), though in each case some problems remain. The Board has had to steer a delicate path between appearing weak and risking offending auditors or finance directors. Its chairman, Sir David Tweedie, has been willing to argue publicly for the Board's views. Probably no group of people could have done the job better; but that leaves open the question whether it is a task that any group of people should be invited to undertake.

The ASB has come under fire for threatening to overwhelm accountants with discussion papers, exposure drafts, financial reporting standards, UITF proposals, chapters of the Statement of Principles, and other odds and ends. The 18 extant standards from the ASC average 12½ pages each including notes and examples. There was no apparent lengthening of standards during the ASC's 20-year life. But the first seven FRSs from the ASB average 55 pages each, including everything. And they do seem to be getting longer. The first four FRS's average 44 pages, the next three 69 pages each.[12] The explanation section of each FRS, which can be extensive, is normally to be 'regarded as part of the statement of standard accounting practice insofar as it assists in interpreting the statement'. The result is that UK accounting standards in issue currently total more than 600 pages.

Company Law

In effect the legal requirements in the Companies Act are accounting standards too, though they are not usually referred to as such. The Cohen Report on Company Law Amendment (1945) led to much expanded accounting disclosure requirements in the Companies Act 1948 (about 26 pages in total). In particular, the 1948 Act required group accounts, and disclosure of many more specific items, and made the profit and loss account subject to audit.

The Jenkins Report on Company Law (1962) led to further disclosure requirements in the Companies Act 1967, for example, on turnover and changes in fixed assets. (The fact that UK company accounts before 1966 hardly ever disclosed such a basic matter as annual turnover constitutes a strong argument at least for some accounting rules on disclosure.)

The Companies Act 1981 began to include measurement rules, in addition to disclosure requirements. It followed SSAP 2 in including general accounting principles: going concern, consistency, prudence and accruals. The 1981 Act also followed the EEC Fourth Directive on Company Law in prescribing a limited number of formats for balance sheets and profit and loss accounts. These differed in some respects from the reporting format that most UK companies already tended spontaneously to follow.

The Companies Act 1985 consolidated five existing Companies Acts. The Companies Act 1989 implemented the EEC Seventh Directive dealing with group accounts and other amendments. The original 1985 Act contained 123 pages dealing with company accounts; but the amended 1985 Act contains 187 pages, more than seven times the volume of legislation in the 1948 Act.

---

[12] The print in my 1995 ICAEW Members' Handbook is a good deal smaller for some FRSs than in the 1994 Handbook; so the number of pages per accounting standard may not be consistent from year to year!

Company law sometimes duplicates and sometimes contradicts normal accounting standards. Many of the specific disclosure requirements either overlap with others or call for pointless detail. There is scope for substantial reduction.[13] Appendix 2 (below, p.67) gives details of seven examples where Schedule 4 of the Companies Act 1985 seems to conflict with accounting standards. There may well be others.

What Accounting Standards Cover

Accounting standards, together with legal requirements in the Companies Act, cover five kinds of requirements: scope, definition, presentation, disclosure and measurement.

(i) *Scope* means the size or kind of entity or transaction to which standards apply. Some standards exclude certain kinds of entity: SSAP 3 exempts banking and insurance companies; SSAP 19 excludes charities; and the Companies Act does not apply to partnerships and sole traders, nor to many non-business entities. And some standards exclude certain kinds of transactions: for example, SSAP 12 on depreciation does not apply to goodwill or to investment properties.

Some standards do not apply to small and medium-sized companies (for example, part of SSAP 13, FRS 1, FRS 2); and the Companies Act (section 247) also makes this distinction where a company meets at least two of the following criteria:

	Small	Medium
Turnover (£ million)	< £2.8	< £11.2
Total assets (£ million)	< £1.4	< £5.6
Employees (number)	< 50	< 250

A recent CCAB working party[14] suggested exempting 'small' companies from all but five accounting standards (SSAPs 4,9,13,17 and 18) and UITF 7. The working party thought it not

---

[13] See, for example, Ernst & Young's *Views on Disclosure in Company Accounts* (December 1992), which makes 50 specific suggestions: 10 for simplification, 25 for deleting company law requirements on disclosure, and 15 for deleting SSAP or FRS requirements.

[14] CCAB Consultative Document, 'Exemptions from Standards on Grounds of Size or Public Interest', November 1994.

worthwhile for small companies to follow any of the standards issued since 1980.

(ii) *Definitions* may partly overlap with scope: for example, SSAP 13 defines 'research' fairly narrowly. Some standards define key terms controversially; for example, 'cash equivalents' in FRS 1, or 'extraordinary items' and 'earnings per share' in FRS 3; or 'current assets' in para.77 of Schedule 4 of the Companies Act.

(iii) *Presentation* rules may refer to required terminology. There are also now detailed formats for accounts (two basic formats to choose from for balance sheets, and four for profit and loss accounts). FRS 1 requires a particular format for cash flow statements, and FRS 3 a new statement of 'total recognised gains and losses'.

(iv) *Disclosure* requirements demand that companies disclose certain matters either in the accounts or in the notes. These may stem from the Companies Act: for example, turnover, acquisitions and disposals of fixed assets, details of tax expense, corresponding amounts for the previous year; or from accounting standards: for example, deferred tax, pensions, cash flow statements. There are two general requirements: to disclose accounting policies in a number of areas (SSAP 2); and to disclose any failure to abide by accounting standards, with reasons (Companies Act, Sch.4, para.36A).

The extent of disclosure, often in the notes, has increased greatly over the last 20 years. Between 1973 and 1993 the number of pages of notes in three large companies' accounts expanded as follows:

	1973	1993
	No. of pages	*No. of pages*
The General Electric Company	7	20
Grand Metropolitan	6	20
Imperial Chemical Industries	8	21

(v) *Measurement* is the final aspect covered by accounting standards - of assets and liabilities or of profit and loss. Measurement standards are often complex, and may be controversial; and they can significantly affect reported results: for example, deferred tax (SSAP 15); foreign currency translation (SSAP 20); pension costs (SSAP 24). In a complicated set of accounts, moreover, drafting the narrative can be as difficult as computing the figures.[15] (This has obvious implications when translating foreign accounts.) The Companies Act contains less on measurement, but lays down rules about including only realised profits, valuing stocks at the lower of cost or net realisable value, and revaluing fixed assets.

Accounting Standards in the USA

In the United States government agencies have influenced the development of accounting standards for listed companies more than in the UK. The Federal Trade Commission (FTC) and the Securities and Exchange Commission (SEC) were both set up in response to crises in the financial markets: the FTC by the Clayton Antitrust Act of 1914, following the credit crisis of 1907, and the SEC in 1934 as part of the government's response to the Great Crash of 1929.

In each case the accounting profession needed to placate a government agency which formally had the power to take over its leading role. So in 1916 there was an agreement with the FTC on uniform accounting methods; and in 1936 the American Institute of Certified Public Accountants (AICPA) set up a new Committee on Accounting Procedure (CAP). This was the first formal 'standard-setting' body, which aimed to narrow the areas of difference in corporate reporting.

The CAP had about 20 part-time unpaid members, mostly in public practice. Its output, 51 advisory Accounting Research Bulletins (ARBs), listed practices which the SEC 'accepted' in filed accounts. In 1959 the Accounting Principles Board (APB), another committee of the AICPA, replaced the CAP and published 31 APB Opinions. Again all its 18 members were unpaid and part-time, though now including some academics and business people.

In the late 1960s there were a number of 'scandals' which (as in the UK) led to a new body. The Financial Accounting Standards Board (FASB), which succeeded the APB in 1973, comprises seven full-time paid members selected by the trustees of the Financial Accounting Foundation. In addition to those ARBs and APB

---

[15] A.M.C. Morison, 'The Role of the Reporting Accountant Today', in W.T. Baxter and Sidney Davidson (eds.), *Studies in Accounting Theory,* London: Sweet & Maxwell, 3rd edn. 1977.

Opinions which continue in existence, it has issued well over a hundred Financial Accounting Standards. (US practice is to issue a new FAS, with a new number, where UK practice amends an existing standard and retains its old number.) The two thick volumes of standards and other pronouncements contain over 3,000 pages.

The FASB is well-funded. Its standards tend to be longer than UK SSAPs (though UK FRSs run them close), and permit few alternatives. In recent years the FASB is thought to have strongly influenced the International Accounting Standards Committee (IASC). Its importance is underlined by US capital markets being the busiest in the world. In general accounting, academics have been more influential on the contents of US accounting and accounting standards than they have been in the UK. It is open to question whether or not this has been helpful.

Accounting Standards in Other Countries

The International Accounting Standards Committee (IASC) started in 1973 with accounting bodies from nine countries. Bodies from over 80 countries are now members. The IASC has been influential in many developing countries and in the emerging economies of Eastern Europe. Until recently most of the IASC's 31 standards followed UK or US standards, often allowing more than one method. In 1993, however, 10 standards were revised with a substantial reduction of options. But the IASC has no means of enforcing its standards.

This paper deals mainly with British standards and to a lesser extent American ones. Both countries have influenced accounting in Australia and Canada which have their own standard-setting bodies. These are the four main countries in the 'Anglo-Saxon' group of countries whose accounting, in several respects, differs from that in Continental Europe and Japan. One key reason has been the much greater importance of public capital markets.

Dutch accounting is well established, with Shell and Unilever two of the leading multinational enterprises. The Council for Annual Reporting publishes both 'definitive pronouncements' and 'recommendations' as guidelines, which companies need not follow (though they usually do). Interested parties may complain to the Court of Justice if they believe that financial statements do not comply with the law. The Enterprise Chamber, comprising three judges and two experts, but no jury, may order correction. Where the Chamber gives reasons for its decisions they may affect the reporting practices of other companies.

French accounting is based on the national accounting code, with a standardised chart of accounts and standard terminology. Provision exists for adapting to the needs of particular industries. The government has had more influence on financial reporting than have the professional accounting bodies. There are no accounting standards of the Anglo-Saxon kind.

German accounting is heavily influenced by tax law. All business entities are subject to the accounting requirements of the Commercial Code, which vary with the legal form of the enterprise. Generally accepted accounting principles - which are not codified - govern financial statements. They stem from various sources: the Chamber of Accountants' recommendations, the Commercial Code, company law, tax law, and business practice. There are no accounting standards of the Anglo-Saxon kind.

Accounting in Japan is influenced by three different government sources: the tax laws; the Commercial Code, under the Ministry of Justice; and the Securities and Exchange Law under the Ministry of Finance. The latter, aided by a Business Accounting Deliberation Council, publishes Business Accounting Principles (standards) which listed companies must follow. The IASC has not made much difference because it aims to work through professional accounting bodies, and the Japanese Institute of Certified Public Accountants has little influence on financial reporting.

A current issue is whether the European Union should attempt to develop its own accounting standards. Given the wide range of varying approaches even within the 15-nation group, from an Anglo-Saxon point of view there seems little useful purpose in inserting another standard-setting body between the IASC and the national bodies. The EU could enforce standards (unlike the IASC), but its pronouncements may not always be 'generally acceptable'.

II. ARGUMENTS FOR AND AGAINST STANDARDS

This section sets out and discusses arguments for and against accounting standards. Many people who favour standards seem to find it hard to explain exactly why, and the same is true of many who oppose them. Both Solomons[1] and the Dearing Committee[2] acknowledged that not everyone favours accounting standards; and even those who do may not agree with every detail of the present arrangements. The second part of the section sets out three arguments against standards. Sections III and IV discuss the purpose of company accounts and the setting and enforcing of standards. The fifth and final section of this *Hobart Paper* gives an overall view of the costs and benefits of accounting standards.

Possible Damage to Investors

'Managers may have more to gain by withholding information than from disclosing it. We cannot depend on the market to discipline promptly companies that are free to choose what and how to report to investors. Even if good accounting can be relied on to drive out bad in the long run, investors may suffer too much damage in the short run to permit freedom from regulation.'[3]

This argument suggests that standards should at least require minimum levels of disclosure, if not particular methods of measurement. But permitting insider dealing would allow stock markets to reflect sooner any news managers possess.

Researchers have reported a number of persistent stock market 'anomalies'.[4] But they do not show whether markets' efficiency has changed, nor what difference, if any, accounting standards

---

[1] David Solomons, 'The Political Implications of Accounting and Accounting Standard Setting', *Accounting and Business Research*, Spring 1983.

[2] ICAEW, *The Making of Accounting Standards*, September 1988.

[3] David Solomons, *op. cit.*, p. 107 (adapted).

[4] Elroy Dimson (ed.), *Stock Market Anomalies*, Cambridge: Cambridge University Press, 1988.

have made. (Accounting standards help determine what is publicly available, rather than how 'efficiently' the market digests it.)[5] There is an extensive American literature on the regulation of accounting,[6] which helps to highlight the issues, although the outcome is remarkably inconclusive. Certainly the various costs of regulation (including opportunity costs) must be set against its benefits before one can begin to infer 'market failure'. But measuring either costs or benefits seems to be extremely difficult.

According to Watts and Zimmerman:

> 'The SEC spends virtually none of its budget in systematically assessing the costs and benefits of regulation.'

Foster says:

> '...it is far from obvious that a policy body such as the SEC or the FASB can regulate information production so as to achieve an efficient allocation of resources...'

And Beaver concludes:

> 'In the absence of evidence, the desirability of having a regulated environment is an open issue.'

Rose[7] suggested that without full disclosure by legal compulsion the check on the way companies use retained profits is likely to be too weak. Another way to control the use of profits might be to let shareholders vote to increase dividends above what company directors recommend. It is possible that accounts might help assess the riskiness of shares in a particular company. But according to modern portfolio theory, investors can largely diversify away such specific risk - by holding a number of different securities - so this hardly seems to justify all the paraphernalia of accounting standards.

Solomons mentions potential damage to investors. Between 1945 and 1969 the ICAEW issued Recommendations to its members, while the Scottish Institute preferred not to. But were

---

[5] I owe this point to an anonymous referee.

[6] William H. Beaver, *Financial Reporting: An Accounting Revolution*, Englewood Cliffs, New Jersey: Prentice-Hall, 2nd edn., 1986, Ch. 6; George Foster, *Financial Statement Analysis*, Prentice-Hall, 2nd edn., 1986, Ch. 2; Ross L. Watts and Jerold L. Zimmerman, *Positive Accounting Theory*, Prentice-Hall, 1986, Ch. 7.

[7] Harold Rose, *Disclosure in Company Accounts*, Eaton Paper No. 1, London: Institute of Economic Affairs, 1963, 2nd edn., 1965, p. 16.

Scottish company accounts therefore of lower quality than English ones? There was little evidence in the United States of fraudulent or misleading financial statements prior to the arrival of legal standards in 1934.[8] So is there any reason to think that absence of accounting standards would have damaged UK investors? If the Solomons suggestion about the long run is correct we might now be better off if 25 years ago we had not introduced accounting standards.

In fact, deliberate action by British governments has caused far more serious damage to investors than any absence of accounting standards. Hence any notion that government interference in accounting is intended or likely to help investors must be open to grave suspicion. Helping investors has not been a high priority for British governments since the Second World War.

For many years UK law required trustees to invest in government securities a large part of the funds under their control. (The Chinese government recently issued a similar edict.) This was supposed to limit risk, but in fact only ensured heavy real losses. Between 1946 and 1961, when the Trustee Investment Act relaxed the rules, the real value of British government securities fell by about 75 per cent. Exchange controls, too, which lingered on for 34 years after the War, trapped British residents between 1939 and 1979 and caused them huge losses.

The British tax system has eviscerated UK investors.[9] For many years before 1979 the top rate of tax on income from investments exceeded 90 per cent. These penal rates of confiscation raised very little revenue for the government to spend on 'good causes'. And capital gains tax, whose net yield was also very small, failed to allow for currency debasement between 1965 and 1982. During this period the pound lost over 80 per cent of its purchasing power. Admittedly, some accountants can hardly complain about the taxation of 'fictional' gains, since they continue to connive at the reporting of fictional profits.

---

8   George J. Benston, 'The Effectiveness and Effects of the SEC's Accounting Disclosure Requirements', in Henry Manne (ed.), *Economic Policy and the Regulation of Corporate Securities*, Washington DC: American Institute for Public Policy Research, 1969.

9   D.R. Myddelton, *The Power to Destroy: a study of the British tax system*, London: Society for Individual Freedom, 2nd edn., 1994.

Pressures on Preparers and Auditors of Accounts

One of the Dearing Committee's reasons for having accounting standards was the pressures to which preparers and auditors of accounts can be exposed. This is not new: preparers of accounts, certainly of listed companies, have always faced pressures. Agents providing an account of their stewardship may well prefer to present a rosy picture rather than a gloomy one.

Standards which require or rule out certain accounting treatments reduce the range of choice about how best to provide 'a true and fair view'. Preventing company directors to some extent from using their judgement may indeed reduce the pressure on them; but that is not to say it will result in accounts of higher quality. To suppose otherwise almost suggests that many company directors are rogues and that many auditors and their firms are pusillanimous.

The existence of accounting standards may help to alleviate two different kinds of 'pressures' on auditors: possible lawsuits for negligence, and client companies threatening to 'shop around' for more congenial audit opinions.[10]

If standards reduce the scope for judgement, auditing may become lower-risk. It may be a sound defence against a lawsuit for negligence to be able to show that a company's accounts have complied with detailed rules. In the absence of standards, a firm of auditors might be less confident of convincing a court that its judgement was not negligent. But in the long run auditing will become a lower-skill, lower-risk job, and fees will fall.

Compulsory standards may help prevent competition in ideas. But why is that fitting for the accounting profession? One needs a low opinion of most auditors' competence and integrity to suppose that, in the absence of standards, bad accounting practices will drive out good. Baxter long ago pointed out that the existence of standards imposes heavy pressures on an auditor's independence of judgement:

> 'Suppose that the medical profession's first dislike of antiseptic surgery had crystallised in a hostile recommendation; that one of Lister's patients had died; and that the deceased's relatives had brought a suit for negligence. What would have been the effect on surgery? Where an auditor is faced with [such a]

---

[10] It makes sense to talk of 'client companies', even though some purists argue that the 'client' is not a company's management but its shareholders.

risk, the temptation to play safe - by abandoning his independence of judgement - is very great.'[11]

It is unlikely to be in a company's long-run interests to attempt to deceive its own members, though it is possible that a board of directors would take a shorter-term view. Nor would auditors gain in the long run if they abetted any such attempt. As Fama writes:

'Like the outside directors, the outside auditors are policed by the market for their services which prices them in large part on the basis of how well they resist perverting the interests of one set of factors (e.g. security holders) to the benefit of other factors (e.g. management). Like the professional outside director, the welfare of the outside auditor depends largely on "reputation".'[12]

Admittedly, this does not guarantee the complete absence of short-term attempts at deception in accounts; but it is doubtful whether any other method can be found to do so either. If audit firms are all reduced to ticking boxes to record compliance with standard rules, they cannot distinguish themselves by the quality of their judgement. Then 'reputation' hardly matters.

Public Expectations of Comparability

'How do you explain to an intelligent public that two companies in the same industry can follow different accounting principles and both get a true and fair audit report?'[13]

'The value of the information which each company provides to its shareholders is much enhanced if it is easy to compare with other companies' accounts. So regulation is needed to secure what everyone wants.'[14]

An intelligent public should recognise a few basic points about accounting:

---

[11] W.T. Baxter, 'Recommendations on Accounting Theory', based on an article in *The Accountant*, 10 October 1953, reprinted in W.T. Baxter and Sidney Davidson (eds.), *Studies in Accounting Theory*, London: Sweet & Maxwell, 2nd edn., 1962, p. 424.

[12] Eugene Fama, 'Agency Problems and the Theory of the Firm', *Journal of Political Economy*, Vol. 88, No. 2, 1980.

[13] Michael Lafferty, 'Why It Is Time for Another Leap Forward', *Accountancy*, January 1979.

[14] David Solomons, *op. cit.*, p.107.

- It is very ambitious to aim to present the complex affairs of large companies in three summary financial statements, even with many pages of notes.

- In a going concern, many transactions are incomplete at the balance-sheet date; hence the annual accounts have to contain estimates as to their future outcome.

- In making estimates about the uncertain future, there are no uniquely 'correct' answers, and competent people may honestly hold different views.

- Different companies, whether or not in the same industry, may quite properly use accounting policies which are not identical.

As Shank writes:

'There is, quite simply, no way to reduce the totality of the complex operations of an on-going multidimensional business organisation into a neat set of accounting calculations. Many aspects of business can't be quantified at all, e.g. employee morale, customer acceptance and management expertise. Many of those aspects which can be quantified do not permit precise measurement...Even those aspects which do yield seemingly precise measures often yield different measures depending on the judgement of the measurer.'[15]

To what extent can the accounts of different companies usefully be compared with each other? Hornstobel refers to the demand for uniformity and rigid rules

'so that security analysts and others can look at the numbers and delude themselves into thinking that they are comparing the operating results and performances of unrelated and wholly different companies. Such comparisons are just not feasible.'[16]

Indeed, users seem to value information that is consistent over time more highly than information that purports to be comparable between two or more companies.[17]

---

[15] John Shank, *op. cit.*, p.87.

[16] Charles C. Hornstobel, 'Speaking Out on Financial Reporting Challenges', *Journal of Contemporary Business*, Spring 1973, p.79.

[17] AICPA Special Committee on Financial Reporting, *Meeting the Information Needs of Investors and Creditors*, AICPA, November 1993.

Certainly comparability over time within one company is much easier. More than 30 years ago I examined the financial results of the five main American cigarette companies over the period 1951-62.[18] But comparing the results of the different companies directly was rarely possible, even though they made almost identical products. Most of the reasons for non-comparability still exist today. Whatever its own approach, any company would have to be consistent in its use over time and to highlight any 'material' change in practice. (This might mean – as in SSAP 3: Earnings per Share – making a difference of 5 per cent or more.) Analysing trends over a period of, say, five years is likely to mean more than examining only a single period's results.

If accounting standards could help achieve comparability between companies, and if that were useful, then in today's international capital markets there should presumably be a single global standard-setter. Yet national standard-setters, in the UK as much as anywhere, seem quite willing on occasions to ignore what other countries do.

The first rule for company accounts should be: *'Caveat lector –* let the reader take care'. The accounting profession should not pander to ignorance by implicitly promising the public something which cannot be delivered. Every company has its unique features; and at best accounts can only give a very approximate impression of performance and financial position. These points deserve emphasis whether or not the present system of standards remains.

The existence of standards tends to raise expectations about the precision and comparability of company accounts above what is feasible. This is partly because of ballyhoo about what standards are attempting to do; and partly because providing for enforcement implies (wrongly) that they can in fact do it. The public cannot be experts on accounting, any more than on brain surgery or atomic physics. (Do we need official 'standards' in those fields too?) If public expectations are too high, then the accounting bodies and others should try to lower them. Education is no doubt important, but it may not be the whole answer. Is it funny or sad that the Conference of Professors of Accounting publishes its annual accounts as if they were accurate to the *nearest penny?*

The present official approach proudly points to a distinguished

---

[18] D.R. Myddelton, 'The Comparability of Published Financial Statements', unpublished research report, Harvard Business School, 1963.

Accounting Standards Board, appointed by a fairly representative Financial Reporting Council, an extensive consultation process, a Review Panel with powers to prosecute offenders, 25 accounting standards in issue and more in the pipeline, an Urgent Issues Task Force which operates even more quickly than the ASB, etc. etc. The clear message is: *'You, the investing public, can safely rely on all this expert effort.'* But, unfortunately, being seen to *attempt* something by no means guarantees its achievement. Meaning well is not the same as doing good.

Complexity of Accounting Decisions

Another of the Dearing Committee's reasons for having accounting standards was the complexity of the decisions faced by preparers and auditors of accounts. Accounting is complex. This is partly to mirror the complex nature of modern business and partly because of the technical character of accounting itself, which intertwines economic and legal concepts. As a result, company directors and auditors must exercise judgement in presenting accounts. It is strange, therefore, to find anyone relying on complexity to support the case for mandatory accounting standards which limit their freedom to do so.

It may well be useful for accounting bodies to offer advice to their members on some technical aspects of preparing accounts. But that need not mean compulsory standards. It can be dangerous to rely on authority to lead to truth. Nazi mathematics and Soviet biology are two infamous examples from science this century. The same is true in accounting. As Stigler says:[19] 'Authority, the equivalent of monopoly power, is the great enemy of freedom of inquiry.'[20]

In some respects standard-setters may have made accounting more complex - for example, SSAP 24 on Pension Costs or the American FAS 109 on tax. The recent ASB discussion paper on goodwill proposing a valuation method called 'Capitalisation and Annual Review' contained an extremely complex 15-page Appendix. (It brought back memories of the 400-page guidance

---

[19] George J. Stigler, *The Intellectual and the Market Place*, IEA Occasional Paper No. 1, London: Institute of Economic Affairs, 1963.

[20] For an opposing view, where the call is for ever-stronger authority, see Michael Bromwich, *The Economics of Accounting Standard Setting*, London: Prentice-Hall/ICAEW, 1985.

manual to ED 18: Current Cost Accounting.)

The ASB sometimes complicates presentation, too, as in FRS 3's hard-to-follow profit-and-loss account layout. And the same standard's Statement of Recognised Gains and Losses may merely reflect confused thinking. This Statement more or less duplicates the details of changes in reserves which the Companies Act already requires. It perpetuates the mixture of historical costs and current values which is a thoroughly bad feature of modern British accounting.

Uniform Words and Layout

'Uniformity, both of words and layout, can help reduce the "semantic noise" which obstructs the clarity of the message.'[21]

This seems rather a minor point: most British readers can follow American balance sheets, even though the format is different, and the only common terms are 'current assets' and 'cash'. It is somewhat ironic that the EC should be dictating which English words to use in accounts. After all, companies in other member-states are using Danish, Dutch, Finnish, French, German, Greek, Italian, Portuguese, Spanish and Swedish!

There is little need for standards to *impose* uniform words and layout. Where this makes sense, it tends to happen anyway. Any official system of language is likely to freeze practice, and can be positively harmful. Most English people know two examples: the imposition of 'newspeak' in Orwell's *Nineteen-Eighty-Four*, which tried to stamp out freedom and restrict thought, and the laughable attempts of the Académie Française to 'purify' French. (Apparently, in place of '*le PE ratio*' is preferred '*le coefficient de capitalisation des résultats*'.[22])

The Fourth Directive required 'current liabilities' to be replaced as a stand-alone item by 'creditors: amounts falling due within one year'. In many balance sheets this now takes up two lines. And some companies continue to include 'current liabilities' as a heading *in addition* to the Euro-speak requirement - which is thus redundant as well as compulsory. The well-known term 'current liabilities' caused no trouble in the UK before it

---

[21] Peter Bird, as quoted by Solomons, *op. cit.*, p.108.

[22] Christopher Nobes and Robert Parker, *Comparative International Accounting*, Hemel Hempstead, Herts.: Prentice-Hall, 4th edn., 1995, p.89.

was outlawed. Was it unsuitable or liable to be misunderstood? Evidently not: for the official line after 'net current assets' reads: 'total assets less current liabilities'.

For another example, the 1989 Companies Act, in amending the 1985 Act, states:

> 'For "related companies", wherever occurring in any other context (than "shares in related companies"), substitute "undertakings in which the company has a participating interest".'

Do we really need this sort of legislation? Here the compulsory change requires nine words in place of two, 20 syllables instead of six. Anyone should be free to use this new term if they prefer it: that, after all, is how language develops. But again, the required expression seems clumsier than the one it replaces.

The question also arises: by what process do we expect gradual improvements over time to occur? Are we to assume that we have already reached perfection? Or will the EC issue new instructions as soon as they become desirable? (It has been suggested that both the Fourth and the Seventh Directives are now somewhat out of date.) More likely, I suspect, it will take at least 10 years. Natural evolution of language can move much more quickly than that, and with a lot less fuss. To use a notorious British accounting term, it is *flexible!*

Stopping Evolution

The process of preparing and exposing standards probably stimulates thinking and discussion about specific accounting topics. But the act of issuing a standard may tend to stop further evolution. Standard-setters should welcome unceasing debate as helping to lead towards better accounting. In practice, however, it may be tempting to want to settle questions 'once and for all'. According to Baxter:

> 'In America, one important experiment was stopped because it offended "accepted accounting principles" ...: The SEC compelled the US Steel Company to amend 1947 depreciation figures based on the current price level, and so prevented all further experiment in this field by companies under SEC control.'[23]

---

[23] W.T. Baxter, *op cit.*, p.423.

In the UK, government insistence on Current Cost Accounting had a similar result with respect to Constant Purchasing Power accounting in the late 1970s. In the United States the SEC for a long time refused to file accounts drawn up in vertical form.[24]

There is also a danger that accountants may abdicate their responsibility for accounts and simply wait for standard-setters to lay down rules. It can take time to agree a standard, so in a fast-changing world this may result in some important voids. For example, how should accounts treat options? There is little incentive for companies to make an effort to solve the problem. Whichever method they choose, the ASB may sooner or later outlaw it. Regulation may make users of accounts irresponsible too, if they over-rely on it to protect them from the consequences of their actions. It recalls Herbert Spencer's remark: 'The ultimate result of shielding men from the effects of folly is to fill the world with fools.'[25]

Four important recent US accounting standards passed only by a bare 4-3 margin:

FAS 52: Foreign Currency Translation 1981 (31 pages)

FAS 87: Employers' Accounting for Pensions 1985 (69 pages)

FAS 89: Financial Reporting and Changing Prices 1986 (43 pages)

FAS 95: Statement of Cash Flows 1987 (44 pages)

How long will it be before the above very lengthy standards are amended? FASB members might well be reluctant to re-open issues that had caused severe problems in reaching a conclusion. Of course, we do not know the views of the present FASB. Those who once opposed a standard might have changed their minds; or new FASB members might disagree with those they replaced. Certainly, the narrow balance of opinion might have shifted. It does seem an arbitrary way to set accounting rules, rather like musical chairs: which accounting method can win the vote when the music stops? There is no guarantee that the music will be played again for many years.

---

[24] R.C. Morris, *Corporate Reporting Standards and the 4th Directive*, Research Committee Occasional Paper, ICAEW, 1975, p.31.

[25] Herbert Spencer, 'State Tamperings with Money and Banks', in *Essays*, Vol.iii, London: Macmillan, 1891, p.354.

In a voluntary régime, people can continue to ponder tricky subjects, and views can change slowly. For example, the UK permits both 'average rate' and 'closing rate' methods of translating profit and loss accounts from foreign currencies. Over many years the balance of practice has been shifting towards the 'average-rate' method. In 1982, about two-thirds of those companies which disclosed a method favoured the 'closing-rate' method; but by 1992 about three-quarters favoured the 'average-rate' method. There has always been a respectable number supporting the minority view at any time. As long as a company is consistent, or clearly discloses if it changes its preferred approach, does it really matter that not all companies use the same method?

Those who think we should allow only one method have to decide which it should be. In 1982, the 'closing-rate' method would probably have won the vote, whereas by 1992 the 'average-rate' method was more popular. Thus a standard issued in 1982 might still be forcing UK companies to use the 'closing-rate' method even though (as we know, with hindsight) by 1992 a clear majority preferred the 'average-rate' method. Do we really wish we had forced companies to continue using a method they have now changed their minds about? If so, how can change come about? Or is freedom to choose important here? If so, why not in respect of many other accounting topics too?

Legitimising Bad Accounting

Gresham's Law, that bad money drives out the good, assumes that government interferes in the market by means of legal tender laws. In a free market for money (rare in human history), good money would tend to drive out the bad. Likewise in a free market for accounting, good accounting would in the long term tend to drive out the bad.[26] The sections of the early Companies Acts dealing with accounts tended to copy existing best practice. How fortunate that commercial accounting in those days was allowed to develop freely.

The existence of standards may legitimise bad accounting practices and prohibit good accounting. Just as Parliament could repeal the Law of Gravity if it chose, so the Companies Act could

---

[26] See Edwin Cannan, *An Economist's Protest*, London: P.S. King, 1927, p.348.

deem the contents of any accounting standard to represent 'excellent accounting'. On difficult questions a standard-setting body may be able to win the vote only through compromise. This may stem from business lobbying (as with goodwill in the UK); or from some government agency imposing the rules (as with railroad accounting in the USA); or from direct government interference (as with inflation accounting in both countries).

On goodwill, there has been intense lobbying by companies wishing to avoid ever having to charge part of the cost of their acquisitions against profit. UK standard-setters have so far been unable to resist this pressure. SSAP 22 on goodwill permits UK companies to follow US requirements (which I prefer): namely, treat purchased goodwill as a fixed asset and amortise its cost against profit over its useful life. Guessing the length of life is often difficult; the best that can be done is consistent use of prudent estimates. But nearly all UK companies follow SSAP 22's 'preferred' treatment and deduct the cost of any purchased goodwill at once from reserves (shareholders' funds).

Company law requires accounts to present a true and fair view of management's stewardship, on a prudent basis. Under stewardship accounting it makes no sense for two successful companies to merge and for their new group accounts suddenly to disclose negative shareholders' funds (as happened, for example, with SmithKline Beecham in 1989). In the absence of an accounting standard which is 'presumed' to help accounts to give a true and fair view, it is doubtful whether SSAP 22's 'preferred' treatment would occur. Thus the standard legitimises *worse* accounting than would otherwise obtain. In this case, at least, the standard does not *require* bad accounting; but many who favour standards dislike any alternative being permitted.

According to Spacek, an American government agency, the Interstate Commerce Commission, permitted worse accounting by railroads than would otherwise have occurred:

> '...railroads are permitted to issue financial statements with woefully inadequate depreciation provisions and reserves - something no other business would dare do. But the Commission rules furnish the authority that enables the public accountant to ignore his professional responsibility in expressing his opinion on the railroad statements.'[27]

---

[27] Leonard Spacek, address at the Harvard Business School, September 1959, reprinted in Sidney Davidson *et al.* (eds.), *An Income Approach to Accounting Theory*, Englewood Cliffs, N.J.: Prentice-Hall, 1964.

Likewise May noted that US agencies had acquired jurisdiction over accounting matters, with adverse results: 'the practices which had become discredited were more general in the regulated industries...'[28]

Standards have also prevented adequate accounting for inflation. The logic of inflation accounting (Constant Purchasing Power (CPP) accounting) is simple. When the purchasing power of money is changing (enough) over time, money amounts at different points in time should be treated as if they were 'foreign' currencies. For purposes of translation CPP accounting uses the Retail Prices Index as an 'exchange rate' over time, as a (reciprocal) measure of the 'general purchasing power of money'. If you buy something for £100 and sell it for $150, you have not made a 'profit' of $50. Nobody would suggest deducting pounds from dollars. In the same way, if you buy something for $_{87}$£100 and sell it for $_{95}$150, you have not made a 'profit' of $_{95}$£50. But some people (including the ASB) do suggest that!

Which is more useful to users of accounts: money or constant purchasing power? When the value of money is stable, money itself is a unit of constant purchasing power. But if the value of money is *not* (roughly) stable over time, then people care more about purchasing power: workers with their wages, children with their pocket-money, pensioners, house-owners, users of accounts. Hence the widespread use of index-linking. In times of inflation, all sensible comparisons of financial amounts over time have to be made, perhaps implicitly, in terms of constant purchasing power. CPP does so explicitly in accounts.[29] There is currently no UK accounting standard on inflation accounting. Thus many UK company accounts now contain a mixture of past costs and current values, expressed in terms of money of different dates. The ASB is content to continue with this nonsense. Again the standards régime legitimises bad accounting.

Another example of a standard involving bad accounting is SSAP 15 on deferred tax. My own view is that there is no link between UK taxable profits and real accounting profits. I therefore prefer the 'flow-through' method, which makes no

---

[28] George O. May, *Financial Accounting: a Distillation of Experience*, London: Macmillan, 1943, p.258.

[29] D.R. Myddelton, *On a Cloth Untrue: Inflation Accounting, the way forward*, Cambridge: Woodhead-Faulkner, 1984.

provision for 'deferred tax'. The UK standard SSAP 15 requires partial provision for deferred tax, excluding timing differences where 'it is probable that a liability or asset will not crystallise'. This stems from 1978 when the corporate tax rate was 52 per cent and there were 100 per cent first-year capital allowances as well as stock relief. A poor standard which at the time may have seemed expedient has remained (despite a 1985 'revision') long after conditions have changed.

SSAP 15's deferred tax 'rule' is highly ambiguous. A recent survey[30] showed a sample of 300 companies providing for a wide variety of proportions of timing differences – hardly the 'comparability' for which the standard-setters pine! It is just possible that everyone interprets SSAP 15 in exactly the same way. The widely varying proportions of timing differences provided for may merely reflect different circumstances. But it seems far more likely that various companies interpret SSAP 15 differently. That rather negates the purpose of a compulsory standard.

Stifling Independent Judgement

Luckily there is no need for academics to allow official accounting standards to override their own judgement. They are still permitted – even encouraged – to think for themselves. What a pity that professional accountants and company directors no longer enjoy such a luxury. What happens if companies or their auditors disagree with the contents of accounting standards? They have to pretend they hold a view even if they do not.

The audit report on UK company accounts normally starts thus:

> 'In our opinion the financial statements give a true and fair view of the state of affairs of the company and the group at the end of the financial year and of the group's profit and cash flows for the year then ended and have been properly prepared in accordance with the Companies Act 1985.'

But are the first three words correct? Are auditors now really giving their own opinions? Or are they just certifying that the accounts accord with accounting standards and with the Companies Act 1985?

Companies and auditors who feel a need for precise rules,

---

30 ICAEW, *Financial Reporting 1990-91: A Survey of UK Reporting Practice*, p.188.

rather than the fuzzier 'spirit' of standards, become experts at hair-splitting. At the extreme such an approach almost implies that if the rules do not prohibit it, anything goes. Accounting starts to emulate tax legislation in its incomprehensible gobbledygook. A few accountants may genuinely agree with the entire contents of each of the 25 extant UK accounting standards, inconsistencies and all. But I doubt if any member of the present Accounting Standards Board does so; or indeed any former standard-setter. Still they all have to follow orders, whatever they think. The 'true and fair override' is not a ploy that can be used routinely.

It is a pity that the term 'creative accounting' has become one of abuse. A number of books have listed dubious accounting practices under this generic title.[31] But there is plenty of legitimate room in accounting for creative thinking in dealing with new conditions – for example, in whether to discount liabilities, or in whether to capitalise finance leases. Accounting is an art, not a science, and trying to outlaw creativity would cripple the profession. Restricting company accountants and auditors to checking compliance with rules is like requiring real artists to behave like small children and paint by numbers!

---

[31] For example, Ian Griffiths, *Creative Accounting*, London: Firethorn Press, 1985; Michael Jameson, *A Practical Guide to Creative Accounting*, London: Kogan Page, 1988; Terry Smith, *Accounting for Growth*, London: Century Business, 1992.

III. THE PURPOSE OF COMPANY ACCOUNTS

Conceptual Framework

In the 1970s the American FASB embarked on its ambitious 'Conceptual Framework' project, which absorbed huge amounts of time and money, and ended in 1985. Its echoes linger on, in the British ASB's 'Statement of Principles', due to appear soon as an Exposure Draft. The idea was driven by a school of academics seeking a comprehensive, self-consistent, 'scientific' deductive system of accounting. This contrasted with the traditional inductive approach which most professional accountants favoured, but under which some practices (and standards) conflict with others.

Solomons[1] thinks such a framework could also help defend accounting from government interference; though constructing it, like standard setting, is itself a political process.[2] Solomons seems to assume that regulators know what 'best' accounting is, and wants their views imposed on everyone. But there is no agreement on what *is* 'best', and even if there were it might not last long.

Why should people want an Accounting Standards Board to dictate standards with which they disagree? The FASB compares accounting standards to traffic laws: it says in the long run those who have to waive their personal preferences to observe common standards will gain more than they lose. According to this expression of faith, each company merely needs to understand correctly its own long-run interest.

But this analogy is false. Where there *needs* to be a single collective approach - as with traffic - most people are willing to accept one. There is no question of a 'personal preference': nobody cares *which* side of the road we drive on as long as, in any given geographic area, we all do the same. (For example, British

---

1 David Solomons, *op. cit.*

2 Pelham Gore, *The FASB Conceptual Framework Project 1973-1985*, Manchester: Manchester University Press, 1992.

drivers, used to driving on the left in their own country, have little difficulty driving on the right in Europe.)

A better analogy with accounting might be a smoking ban even where some people want to be able to smoke. It would be absurd to claim that every single smoker 'gains' from such a ban. And in most cases no complete ban is necessary. It is perfectly feasible, for example, to have 'smoking' compartments at both ends of a train, and 'non-smoking' ones in the middle; though they do need to be clearly marked.

If directors and auditors think a particular accounting treatment gives a true and fair picture of events in a specific case, why should standard-setters forbid such a treatment? Tolerance, openness to different views, competition as Hayek's 'discovery process', all argue for freedom to differ where those responsible think it right. There is a case, however, for requiring companies to disclose clearly which treatment they have chosen.

Most comment on the FASB's Conceptual Framework Project has been critical. Anthony has said: 'There are only a few fundamental issues in financial accounting. The FASB ducked them all.'[3] A recent study says: 'Superlatives have been applied to its inputs, but not to its outputs.'[4] Similar efforts in other countries appear to have no more prospect of success. Indeed, not everyone would regard 'success' as desirable!

No single model of accounting satisfies preparers, auditors, users and academics. Probably least imperfect, in my view, is the stewardship model, based on recoverable historical cost. It is fairly objective, it developed over a long period, and it was widely accepted as relevant before any formal accounting standards existed. This contrasts with the modern attempt by academics to impose a system based on 'decision-usefulness' which sometimes seems to suggest that accounts of the past can or ought to help predict the future.

Stewardship

George O. May, for many years the senior partner of Price Waterhouse in New York, contrasted

---

[3]   R.N. Anthony, 'We don't have the accounting concepts we need', *Harvard Business Review*, January-February 1987, p.75.

[4]   Pelham Gore, *op. cit.*, p.1.

'those who would continue to regard financial statements as reports of progress or of stewardship, and those who would treat them as being in the nature of prospectuses'.[5]

This argument continues today, more than 50 years later, though the Companies Act clearly distinguishes between prospectuses (Part III) and company accounts (Part VII). Most companies only rarely issue a prospectus, which aims to solicit funds directly from the public; but all listed companies publish accounts every year.

Traditionally, company accounts have served as reports to shareholders on the stewardship of directors. Despite important differences between American and British accounting, both stem from the same tradition and are subject to similar pressures. In both countries the increasing separation of corporate management and ownership has made financial statements essential for appraisal of management's actions by shareholders. In 1952 the ICAEW's Recommendation N 15 said:

'The primary purpose of the annual accounts of a business is to present information to the proprietors, showing how their funds have been utilised and the profits derived from such use.'[6]

In 1973 the President of the (US) Financial Executives Institute summarised the orthodox American view:

'The primary purposes of the financial statements of a business enterprise are: (1) to discharge management's obligation to report on its stewardship of the business to its stockholders, and (2) to provide the investing public with meaningful information which can be used to appraise the company's performance.'[7]

In later years the FEI was sharply critical of FASB statements which departed from this line.

Gore claims that the discussion of stewardship in the FASB Conceptual Framework project was confused:

'... in the Trueblood Report ... accountability was taken to imply a duty to use the assets of the company to their best advantage, whereas stewardship simply meant to maintain them... [As was said] the parable of the talents had the same idea and

---

[5]   George O. May, *op. cit.*, p.21.

[6]   ICAEW, 1952, para.1.

[7]   Charles C. Hornstobel, *op. cit.*, p.78.

explained it rather better. Accountability was adopted by the FASB in Tentative Conclusions, but later on ... the word stewardship replaced it, even though the discussion of the concept under consideration remained constant. Thus, the meaning of stewardship was either being silently broadened or the issues confused.'[8]

The legal position seems clear: it supports the stewardship view. In 1965 counsel's opinion (for the ICAEW) was that

'in law the object of annual accounts is to assist shareholders in exercising control of the company by enabling them to judge how its affairs have been conducted.'[9]

The House of Lords repeated this view in the 1990 Caparo case.[10] Lord Jauncey said:

'... the purpose of annual accounts, so far as members are concerned, is to enable them to question the past management of the company, to exercise their voting rights ... and to influence future policy and management.'

And Lord Oliver said:

'I see no grounds for believing that, in enacting the statutory provisions, Parliament had in mind the provision of information for the assistance of purchasers of shares or debentures in the market.'

Historical Cost

In 1962 the Jenkins Committee[11] concluded that the historical cost approach should continue to be the basis for company accounts, as it had been for many years. More recently in the UK, governments and others have enthused about various (often untested) versions of current value accounting. Whatever their potential advantages they suffer, as a rule, by being hypothetical and subject to wide margins of error. (The name 'current cost

---

[8] Gore, *op. cit.*, p.67.

[9] *The Corporate Report*, p.34: a discussion paper published by the Accounting Standards Steering Committee, London, 1975.

[10] Caparo Industries plc *v.* Dickman and others, House of Lords, 8 February 1990, Jauncey, p.49; Oliver, p.40, of 50-page judgement.

[11] *Report of the Company Law Committee* (Jenkins Committee), Cmnd. 1749, London: HMSO, 1964, para. 333.

accounting' coined by Sandilands was a brilliant stroke of public relations as it seems to combine up-to-date-ness with reliability.) Historical cost accounting, in contrast, has sometimes seemed rather old hat; yet it has remained the basis for accounting in the United States and in most other countries.

Ijiri has argued that, for purposes of stewardship, historical cost accounting is better than any current value system.[12] It is the only method which keeps track of an entity's resources; and it is less costly to operate and provides data which are less disputable. Indeed, even the Sandilands Committee pointed out its many important advantages 'when prices are stable' (whatever that is supposed to mean):

> '... historic cost accounting rests on a principle that is readily intelligible to the user of accounts because it is firmly based on the traditional common view that profit is the excess of revenues over historic expenditure. Centuries of use have also resulted in it being well established throughout industry and commerce and its reliance on normally verifiable figures of historic cost means that it is cheap ... compared with other systems of accounting. ... there is no doubt that overall, when prices are stable, historic cost accounting meets the majority of the requirements for information ... Historically this system has proved to be of great value in protecting the interests of shareholders and creditors of companies, and, when prices are stable, results in a clear and unambiguous view of a company's affairs.'[13]

A recent Scottish Institute discussion document[14] suggested that Net Realisable Value might be more relevant as the basis for valuing assets in the balance sheet. Historical cost accounting, though probably more objective, failed the test of additivity completely 'because pounds ... of different dates ... are being added together'. This complaint is true of conventional money cost but not of Constant Purchasing Power (CPP) accounting, which uses the Retail Prices Index to index money costs. CPP

---

[12] Yuji Ijiri, 'A Defence for Historical Cost Accounting', in Robert R. Sterling (ed.), *Asset Valuation and Income Determination*, Scholars Book Company, 1971.

[13] *Report of the Inflation Accounting Committee* (Sandilands), Cmnd. 6225, London: HMSO, September 1975, paras.271 and 273.

[14] Institute of Chartered Accountants of Scotland, P. McMonnies (ed.), *Making Corporate Reports Valuable*, London: Kogan Page, 1988, pp.58-59.

thus manages to overcome the unfitness of money as the unit of account in a period of inflation while retaining all historical cost's many advantages. Perhaps members of the Scottish Institute overlooked the ICAEW's Recommendation N15 which pointed out that constant purchasing power accounting 'is not strictly a proposal for a change from accounting based on historical cost'.[15]

'Decision-Usefulness'

The American Accounting Association (of academics) proposed in 1966 a switch away from stewardship reporting and towards using accounting for economic decision-making.[16] Soon afterwards the (US) Trueblood Report[17] suggested that financial statements should help investors to predict, compare and evaluate potential cash flows to them in terms of amount, timing and related uncertainty. This led on to a statement in the first part of the FASB's Conceptual Framework:

> 'Financial reporting should provide information that is useful to present and potential investors and creditors and other users in making rational investment, credit and similar decisions.'[18]

Other 'conceptual framework' discussions have also suggested 'decision-usefulness' as the main purpose of financial reporting.[19] But the studies themselves usually cite no empirical evidence either about decisions or about users.[20] According to Gore,[21] the FASB adopted a normative, deductive, decision-usefulness approach without properly considering alternatives.

---

[15] ICAEW, Recommendation N15: 'Accounting in relation to changes in the purchasing power of money', May 1952, para.21.

[16] American Accounting Association, *A Statement of Basic Accounting Theory*, 1966.

[17] AICPA, *Report of the [Trueblood] Study Group on the Objectives of Financial Statements*, 1973.

[18] FASB, *Objectives of Financial Reporting by Business Enterprises*, 1978.

[19] In particular, ASSC: 'The Corporate Report', 1975; ICAS, 'Making Corporate Reports Valuable', 1988; ICAEW, 'Framework for the Preparation and Presentation of Financial Statements', 1989 (Solomons).

[20] Michael J. Mumford, 'Users, characteristics and standards', in M.J. Mumford and K.V. Peasnell (eds.), *Philosophical Perspectives on Accounting*, London: Routledge, 1993.

[21] Pelham Gore, *op. cit.*

The three British academics who later became members of the UK Accounting Standards Board all liked the decision-usefulness approach. Carsberg, who had advised the American FASB, admitted[22] that the FASB conceptual framework's findings were mostly assertions with no supporting evidence. Tweedie and Whittington[23] accepted the broad consensus on the purpose of financial reports which all these documents share (listed in note 19).

Most of these conceptual framework efforts outline what their authors think company accounts *ought* to be aiming at. In focussing on decision-usefulness rather than stewardship they seem to be deliberately trying to get away from what most people think company accounts actually are trying to achieve.[24] Similar criticisms of the AICPA's Accounting Research Studies 1 and 3 in the early 1960s halted further work on them.

The accounts of non-business organisations can hardly be useful to investors in making decisions. So the 'decision-usefulness' school has to argue that the purpose of accounting differs as between business and non-business entities. Others may prefer Anthony's view[25] that the primary focus of accounting in both kinds of organisation is on measuring net income to report the extent of success in maintaining financial capital. Therefore accounting practices should be broadly the same.

FAS 117 on the financial statements of not-for-profit organisations states that external financial reporting should focus on the interests of present and potential resource providers. They want to know about organisation performance and management stewardship. On Anthony's view, stewardship reporting can remain the primary purpose of accounts, both for business and

---

[22] Bryan Carsberg, 'The US Conceptual Framework for Financial Reporting' (Lecture at Cardiff, February 1982), in *Contemporary Issues in Accounting*, Bath: Pitman Publishing, 1984, p.106.

[23] David Tweedie and Geoffrey Whittington, 'Financial Reporting: Current Problems and their Implications for Systematic Reform', *Accounting and Business Research*, No.81, Winter 1990.

[24] In 1976 the FASB carried out a survey to determine how many people agreed with Trueblood objectives. According to Dopuch and Sunder (*Accounting Review*, January 1980), it surprised the Board to learn that only 37 per cent of the respondents believed that providing information useful for making economic decisions was an objective of financial accounting.

[25] Robert N. Anthony, *Should Business and Non-business Accounting be Different?*, Cambridge, Mass.: Harvard Business School Press, 1989.

for non-business entities.

In the UK, the Companies Act requires company accounts to provide financial information to its existing shareholders *as a class*. Apart from possibly voting to reduce a proposed dividend (which never happens in practice), the only 'investment' decisions open to the shareholders as a class are whether or not to wind up the company and whether or not to accept a takeover bid. Few people would argue that it is a primary purpose of annual company accounts to assist with the former decision, and I doubt if accounts help much with the latter.

Benston, after a wide-ranging discussion, concluded that the evidence does not suggest that published annual financial statements are useful for investment decisions.[26] They might, however, confirm what investors had learned from other sources.[27] This should be no surprise: company accounts report on what has happened in the past, whereas people making economic decisions care mainly about the *future*. Agency theory clearly implies that stewardship reporting mainly affects the behaviour not of *owners* but of *managers*.[28] It represents a way to monitor the actions of agents in the interests both of agents (managers) and of principals (shareholders).[29] It pays insiders to provide assurance to outsiders.

Even naïve investors can hardly expect to outsmart the rest of the market. But as a rule they can trust the market: they can buy and sell shares at 'fair' prices. And they should also *diversify* their portfolio, either directly or by means of holdings in unit trusts or investment trusts. In practice, naïve investors need hardly bother with a company's annual report and accounts at all, as professional investors and fund managers will be keeping a sharp eye on management's stewardship. Nor are accounts by any means the only source of information for shareholders or stock markets. Indeed, accounts are usually neither the most important nor the most up-to-date source.

---

[26] George J. Benston (1969), *op. cit.*, p.140.

[27] See K.V. Peasnell, 'The Usefulness of Accounting Information to Investors', ICRA, Lancaster, 1973.

[28] Michael Page, 'The ASB's Proposed Objective of Financial Statements: Marching in Step Backwards?', *British Accounting Review*, Vol. 24, March 1992.

[29] See Michael C. Jensen and William H. Meckling, 'Theory of the Firm: Managerial Behaviour, Agency Costs and Ownership Structure', *Journal of Financial Economics*, Vol.3, 1976.

Predicting Future Results

According to the FASB's Conceptual Framework,[30] past account-ing earnings provide a better basis than past cash flows for predicting an enterprise's future cash flows. The evidence for this assertion is unclear. If predicting future cash flows is the primary purpose of accounts, does it imply that the more companies smooth earnings the better? Some accounting standards – on deferred tax and on pensions, for example – do have precisely such an effect, though FRS 3 points strongly in the opposite direction. Stewardship reporting in the Anglo-Saxon countries has long frowned on the practice of 'smoothing' earnings. Accrual accounting itself (as opposed to cash accounting) aims to match expenses suitably against revenues where possible, not to 'smooth' reported profits.

In the 1931 Royal Mail Steamship case[31] the company drew on secret reserves to convert an 'actual' loss into a reported profit. Lord Kylsant (chairman) and Mr Moreland (auditor) were both acquitted on the charge of wilfully deceiving the shareholders. This was probably due to evidence of widespread similar accounting at that time. But practice in this respect changed for the better long before there were formal accounting standards in the UK.

The Sandilands Committee distinguished between 'operating gains' (the excess of current sales revenue over 'current costs') and 'holding gains' (increases in assets' current replacement costs). Sandilands claimed that for most companies the annual operating gains 'may well provide a useful guide' to the company's long-run future earnings.[32] This amazing assertion was not further justified, nor, surely, could it be. That would be even more obvious if accounting profits did not include a 'normal' rate of return on shareholders' funds. Business profits and losses depend on the success of speculation about an *uncertain* future. At least Edwards and Bell, who made a similar statement,[33] recognised that it was

[30] FASB, 'Objectives of Financial Reporting by Business Enterprises', 1978.

[31] Sir Patrick Hastings, 'The Case of the Royal Mail', reprinted in W.T. Baxter and Sidney Davidson (eds.), *Studies in Accounting Theory*, London: Sweet & Maxwell, 2nd edn., 1962.

[32] *Report of the (Sandilands) Inflation Accounting Committee*, Cmnd. 6225, London: HMSO, 1975, para.168.

[33] Edgar O. Edwards and Philip W. Bell, *The Theory and Measurement of Business Income*, Berkeley, California: University of California Press, 1961, p.103 (note 5).

rather unrealistic to assume that production processes will not change.

In 1847 the directors of the Peninsular and Orient Company argued that

> 'Proprietors at a distance forming their opinion of the future position of the company from published accounts of past transactions could scarcely avoid arriving at erroneous conclusions.'[34]

There was, of course, much less disclosure in company accounts 150 years ago than there is today. (Indeed, the passage quoted was used by the company to justify not publishing accounts at all!) But it still seems unlikely that accounts reporting on past performance and financial position can help much in forecasting an enterprise's future cash flows.

As Beaver explains, if a market is efficient:

> 'no amount of security analysis, based on published financial statement data, will lead to abnormal returns [for an investor]...The FASB should actively discourage investors' beliefs that accounting data can be used to detect overvalued or undervalued securities.'[35]

Most studies conclude that annual earnings appear to follow a random walk; hence that past earnings growth does not help predict future growth.[36] Foster calls this result 'one of the most robust empirical findings in the financial statement literature'.[37] The fact is that fundamental analysis of accounting reports is not 'useful' to investors in predicting the future in detail.

---

[34] Quoted in Guy Naylor, *Company Law for Shareholders*, Hobart Paper No. 7, London: Institute of Economic Affairs, 1960, p.12.

[35] William H. Beaver, 'What Should be the FASB's Objectives?', *Journal of Accountancy*, August 1973.

[36] See R. Watts and R. Leftwich, 'The Time Series of Annual Accounting Earnings', *Journal of Accounting Research*, Autumn 1977.

[37] G. Foster, *Financial Statement Analysis*, Englewood Cliffs, N.J.: Prentice-Hall, 2nd edn., 1986, p.240.

IV. SETTING AND ENFORCING STANDARDS

There appear to be four main contenders for the job of setting accounting standards and (if need be) enforcing them:

- professional accounting bodies;
- stock exchanges;
- representative boards; and
- government agencies.

This section discusses both compulsory standards ('Instructions') and voluntary standards ('Suggestions'). Three of the contenders could issue Instructions: stock exchanges because they have powerful means of enforcing them, and representative boards and governments because most people would regard them as politically legitimate. Lacking either attribute, professional accounting bodies would probably be able to issue only Suggestions.

Professional Accounting Bodies

Nearly all preparers of company accounts, and all auditors, are accountants by profession, as are many who 'use' accounts on behalf of those investing funds. For views about medicine, one goes to doctors; about buildings, to architects; so for views about accounting, it seems sensible to go to accountants. There seems little point in aiming for a more 'representative' body to issue voluntary Suggestions. That need relates less to the quality of 'standards' than to the need for political legitimacy to allow *enforcement* of compulsory Instructions. No doubt accounting bodies would seek a wide spread of advice in issuing Suggestions.

Each professional accounting body could (if it chose) issue its own Suggestions to its own members. Indeed, such competition might be healthy in preventing Suggestions from carrying too much 'authority'! It would keep the way open for practice to evolve. It would also emphasise the responsibility of directors for company accounts, and of auditors for their opinions thereon. No doubt on some topics different accounting bodies would be able to agree, but probably not on all.

[48]

The International Accounting Standards Committee could retain its well-known acronym (IASC), and become the International Accounting Suggestions Committee! The process of moving towards harmonisation in accounting (as in much else) is bound to take many years; and a clearly voluntary approach may reduce the pressure for imperfect compromises. Over time the number of different accounting practices in some areas will decline (while in others it may even increase for a time). Permitting some choice may turn out to be a better way to improve accounting than trying to suppress dissent. In the long run, monopoly provision of compulsory accounting standards may be less effective than allowing competition in ideas.

Stock Exchanges

Stock exchanges are probably not the proper bodies to establish accounting practice, since the vast majority of companies are small and unlisted. On the other hand, it may well be that, on cost/ benefit grounds, some standards should apply only to larger listed companies. Stock exchanges might have a role in producing such standards. For smaller companies, shorter and simpler standards might often suffice - or even none at all. A recent ICAEW working party[1] has proposed exempting small companies from all but five accounting standards. (I would allow exemption from *all* accounting standards for both small and medium-sized companies.)

There are at least three different kinds of shareholders, whose needs with respect to company accounts may well differ:

(i) sophisticated investors in listed companies, such as pension funds, analysts;

(ii) small investors in listed companies;

(iii) investors in unlisted companies.

It is the first group at which accounting standards are directly aimed, although the second group may be affected too, perhaps unawares. Whether accounting standards are relevant for the third group seems highly doubtful.

The Companies Act requires all company accounts to give 'a true and fair view', and stock exchanges should not require more.

---

[1] CCAB Working Party, *Exemptions from Standards on Grounds of Size or Public Interest*, November 1994.

The market might value extra details in respect of certain industries, for example, gold mining and oil exploration; but companies could be free to supply it or not as they chose (if their shareholders agreed). The incentive would be a higher share price and/or a better credit rating.

Even an audit has not always been thought essential for very large companies. Alfred P. Sloan reports[2] advising Mr Durant, the founder of General Motors, in 1919 that he thought General Motors should have an independent audit, in view of the large public interest in the corporation's shares. GM's sales in that year were over $500 million.

Stock exchanges possess the power of enforcement, in that they can refuse to list the shares of companies which fail to follow accounting standards. Whether a stock exchange should possess the power to exclude like this is perhaps open to question. This power could apply world-wide: there is extensive discussion between the International Accounting Standards Committee and the International Organisation of Securities Commissions (IOSCO). Not all countries require company accounts to give 'a true and fair view'; but IASC Suggestions could be a useful guide.

Neither the Companies Act nor any accounting standard requires companies to publish interim accounts more frequently than once a year. (In a sense, even annual accounts are only 'interim' for a going concern.) This is the main UK accounting requirement which stems solely from the stock exchange. In the context of stewardship reporting, interim accounts more frequently than once a year may be of little value. Certainly the shorter the period of the profit and loss account, the larger the percentage margin of error in reported profits. A more useful interim measure might be regular quarterly dividends, along US lines, in place of the normal UK practice of irregular 'interim' and 'final' dividends. This would both clarify and make more frequent the 'signal' from management to shareholders.

Representative Boards

In recent years a view has emerged that standard-setting bodies (or at least the group that *appoints* the standard-setters) ought to include users of accounts as well as preparers and auditors. This

---

[2]   Alfred P. Sloan, *My Years with General Motors*, Harmondsworth, Mddx.: Penguin Books, 1986, p.25.

view is probably stronger in the United States than elsewhere. Even so, there appears to be no obvious 'user' currently on the FASB – unless one counts a retired employee of the SEC. But 'users' of accounts surely means *investors*, not bureaucrats. Despite the lip-service that standard-setters pay to the 'needs of users', it is not at all clear what users do expect from accounts.

It may be difficult in practice to ensure that standard-setting boards include all important interests and opinions. For example, it might be hard to persuade someone to serve, even part-time, who did not think Instructions were a good idea. Perhaps the aim should be to maximise the chance or extent of *disagreement* within the board! That might be a convincing test of 'general acceptability'. The alternative might be a self-selecting clique sharing a minority view which they attempt to impose on everyone else.

Standard-setters need to consult widely, to try to gain acceptance. That is important when it comes to enforcing Instructions. An Instruction-issuing board has to market standards as well as produce them. Indeed, Instruction-setting can be highly political, possibly[3] even involving deliberate ambiguities in the language of accounting standards or supporting documents so as to be acceptable to those holding diametrically opposed views. A recent UK example might be the failure, in the ASB's discussion document on goodwill, to specify under precisely what 'special and limited circumstances' companies could use the novel 'capitalisation and annual review method'. The subsequent working paper[4] continues to fudge the issue, presumably on purpose.

George Soros provides a useful reminder of the fallibility of regulators:

> '... regulators are also participants. There is a natural tendency to regard them as superhuman beings who somehow stand outside and above the economic process and intervene only when the participants have made a mess of it. That is not the case. They also are human, all too human. They operate with imperfect understanding and their activities have unintended consequences. Indeed, they seem to adjust to changing

---

[3]   See, for instance, Gore, *op. cit.*, p.103.

[4]   Accounting Standards Board, *Goodwill & Intangible Assets*, working paper for discussion at public hearing, June 1995.

circumstances less well than those who are motivated by profit and loss, so that regulations are generally designed to prevent the last mishap, not the next one.'[5]

The way an Instruction-issuing board works can make a difference. For example, who appoints members of the board? Who sets the agenda? What majority is needed to issue an Instruction? What happens if new members of the board disagree with the view of former members? Are they still stuck with an Instruction which could not now gain sufficient acceptance? If only one accounting method is allowed, there may be rather an abrupt transition when the party line changes. Method A may be required one day, but forbidden the next and Method B required. In contrast, a free market might work more smoothly as well as more quickly (and, of course, less coercively).

There is also the question whether the FASB, consisting of seven full-time paid members, could choose to do nothing in return for their pay. Or must they go on issuing and revising accounting standards even if, for the time being, they think their work is more or less complete? Is the FASB a 'venture' for accounting purposes, or a 'going concern' with an infinite life?

The old UK Accounting Standards Committee had no 'teeth': a qualified audit report, or a possible reprimand from a professional accountant's Institute, were regarded as too mild. Now the Review Panel can take court proceedings against any company whose accounts it believes fail to provide a true and fair view. (So far the Review Panel has always managed to get agreement without actually going to court.) Thus the ultimate sanction is to trigger the *government's* enforcement procedure, under the Companies Act. Some of the ASB's proposals, however, are voluntary, for example, the Operating and Financial Review.

Government Agencies

Given a flourishing UK accounting profession, why should the government take on itself the task of issuing Instructions in accounting which is what it does in the extensive legislation in the Companies Act? Clearly it can muster the powers of enforcement, at least on paper. But does the British government really have a comparative advantage in accounting? In an area where the

---

5   George Soros, *The Alchemy of Finance*, London: Weidenfeld & Nicolson, 1988, p.85.

essential requirements are financial competence and integrity, this seems unlikely.

1994 was rather a special year: the occasion when the British government finally decided to switch over from cash to accrual accounting - well over a century after commercial accounting did so. Far from leading the way in accounting, the government has been using its coercive powers to hold back people who wanted to make this sensible change years ago. 1994 also saw the 25th anniversary of the state monopoly Post Office (then including telephones) first having independent professional accountants audit its annual accounts. (Before then, the Auditor-General, a civil servant, undertook the job.) The result was an eloquent comment on the quality of public sector accounting: no less than two full pages of one of the most heavily-qualified audit opinions in living memory.

In the market there is often a clear benefit from *potential* competition. So also there may be a clear cost from *potential* government interference. It seems certain that governments' notorious propensity to meddle has sometimes led accounting bodies to take otherwise superfluous pre-emptive action - for instance, starting to issue accounting standards.

In the United States, the SEC adds an important element of explicit compulsion. Its Accounting Series Release No.4 (1938) stated that financial statements which are prepared in accordance with accounting principles for which there is 'no substantial authoritative support' will be presumed to be misleading or inaccurate. As Watts and Zimmerman have pointed out, ASR 4 thus created a demand for some means to provide 'substantial authoritative support'.[6] Indeed, they claim that the SEC's role was always to reform existing accounting practice, hence it required accounting principles which do not describe existing practice.

In 1973 ASR No. 150 stated that:

> '...principles, standards and practices promulgated by the FASB will be considered by the Commission as having substantial authoritative support, and those contrary to such FASB promulgations will be considered to have no such support.'

Such an authoritarian approach might not suit every accountant. Suppose you sided with the minority in respect of an accounting

---

[6] Ross L. Watts and Jerold L. Zimmerman, 'The Demand for and Supply of Accounting Theories: The Market for Excuses', *The Accounting Review*, April 1979.

standard issued after a 4-3 decision. Your view would be effectively outlawed, and there would be little chance of getting the standard changed in less than 10 years.

The Chief Accountant of the SEC's Enforcement Division said in 1987:

> 'The essence of professionalism in accounting is the ability to exercise an independent judgement, even when that judgement runs counter to the client's wishes, and especially where the judgement cannot be supported by a clear statement in the literature.'[7]

Fine words; but what about the requirement for 'substantial authoritative support'?[8] In practice it hardly seems that the SEC encourages – or even permits – the exercise of independent professional judgement by American accountants.

Political Interference:
The Case of Inflation Accounting

The UK debate over inflation accounting illustrates the nature and effect of political interference in accounting. It is worth briefly telling the story (whose details are fairly well-known), as a dreadful warning of what *not* to do.

During the late 1960s the annual rate of UK inflation rose towards double figures. In August 1968 the ICAEW published a pamphlet entitled *Accounting for Stewardship in a Period of Inflation* showing *how* to adjust accounts to allow for inflation. Clearly on this sensitive topic it would be both important and difficult to carry opinion with any specific proposal. But at this stage, when approached, the government said it preferred to leave the problem of inflation accounting to the profession to solve.[9]

In August 1971 the ASSC published a Discussion Paper on Inflation and Accounts. In January 1973, after extensive consultation,

---

[7] R.J. Sack, quoted in Alister K. Mason, 'Professional judgement and professional standards', in M.J. Mumford and K.V. Peasnell (eds.), *Philosophical Perspectives on Accounting*, London: Routledge, 1993, p.39.

[8] As ASR 150, quoted above, puts it.

[9] D.S. Morpeth, 'Developing a Current Cost Accounting Standard', in Ronald Leach and Edward Stamp (eds.) *British Accounting Standards: The First 10 Years*, Cambridge: Woodhead-Faulkner, 1981, p.44.

and with the agreement of the CBI, the ASSC published Exposure Draft 8 proposing Current Purchasing Power (CPP) accounting (which I prefer to call Constant Purchasing Power accounting). The government did not like it, and in July 1973 announced it would set up a committee to look into the problem, with Francis Sandilands as chairman. The government's eventual terms of reference emphasised relative price changes as well as general inflation.

The Sandilands Committee's Membership

After six more months of raging inflation the names of the 12 members of the Sandilands Committee were announced. Two of the three accountants had no special interest in the subject: in order to get a 'fresh and uncommitted view', the committee was to exclude any accountants who had expressed a view on the subject. The third accountant member was Michael Inwards – who was a keen supporter of replacement cost accounting! Thus the committee membership was biased from the start. This seems unlikely to have been an accident.

Nine members were not even accountants. As Stamp said:

> '[A]ccounting standards ... cannot be left to amateurs ... If the constructors who constructed a fine hotel had entrusted the installation of its electrical system to a gang of twelve people composed of three electricians, six company directors, an economist, a lady, and the ex-Secretary General of the TUC, it would not surprise me if the management received a shock when they turned the lights on.'[10]

In the event the Sandilands Committee rejected CPP and proposed a form of replacement cost accounting called Current Cost Accounting (CCA), which completely ignored general inflation. This was surprising, in that between July 1973 and September 1975 when the Sandilands Committee published its report, the UK Retail Prices Index rose by no less than 50 per cent! The Sandilands Report's anti-CPP arguments were pathetically thin.[11] Para.414 even argued that the constant purchasing power unit would 'not have a constant value in terms

---

[10] E. Stamp, as quoted in Mason, *op. cit.*, p.33.

[11] See D.R. Myddelton, *On a Cloth Untrue: Inflation Accounting, the way forward*, Cambridge: Woodhead-Faulkner, 1984, Ch.3: 'Sandilands and CPP'.

of the monetary unit' – an astonishing criticism for the self-styled Inflation Accounting Committee to make.

The government demanded a response from the accounting bodies within just over two months. This was not long to consider a CCA system very different from the CPP system which the accountants themselves had proposed. We shall never know what would have happened if the professionals had rejected the Sandilands CCA proposals outright. Like the whole CCA system, it is hypothetical. Clearly it would have been awkward for the government; but it might have been good for accounting and for the independence of the profession.

Current Cost Accounting Standard

In the event, on learning of the profession's response ('modified rapture!'), the government then *instructed* the ASC to produce an accounting standard based on CCA. At no stage in the next 10 years did the government say anything other than: 'Implement a form of CCA'. In particular, the government did not invite the profession, in the light of the Sandilands Report, to choose the best of the rival methods.

In due course the CCA Guidance Manual appeared – more than 400 pages long. It was not popular! In 1977 the members of the ICAEW passed a resolution saying they did not wish any system of Current Cost Accounting to be compulsory. But their views were ignored. The question of 'general acceptability' no longer applied, and over the next few years a series of CCA proposals appeared. ED 18 was abandoned due to complexity; the Hyde Guidelines were only a stop-gap; and ED 24, a revised exposure draft, led, after further changes, to SSAP 16, which finally appeared in 1980.

The CCA standard SSAP 16 was needlessly complex and technically flawed. Many companies soon simply ignored it, with the connivance of their auditors, even though it was supposed to be mandatory (as SSAP 7 never was). Thus, although the government appeared to have the power to enforce its preferred approach to inflation accounting, in the event this proved an illusion.

Thanks to government interference, after a decade of rapid inflation, there was less agreement on inflation accounting at the end than there had been at the beginning. Thus the politicians, of both main parties, helped to bring into disrepute the whole process of private sector accounting standard-setting. As so often when we seem to see a spotlight on 'market failure', behind the scenes the real villain is interference by *government*. Indeed, it was fear of precisely this which induced the accountants to start issuing 'standards' (rather than merely Recommendations) in the first place. The government itself, of course, was also responsible for debasing the currency, which was the initial cause of the problem.

The main good that has resulted, though at a high cost indeed, is a stronger than ever repugnance towards political interference in accounting. But some statesmen remained invincibly ignorant. At the 1983 Annual Conference of the ICAEW, a guest speaker attacked the accounting profession for not solving the problem of accounting for inflation. Who was it? None other than Edward Heath, Prime Minister in the government which had sabotaged the accountants' CPP proposal.

V. CONCLUSIONS

Instructions

Section II outlined arguments for and against compulsory accounting standards ('Instructions'). Arguments for include:

- limiting the risk of potential damage to investors;
- reducing pressures on preparers and auditors of accounts;
- meeting public expectations regarding accounts;
- helping to cope with complex accounting decisions; and
- bringing about uniform words and layout.

Most of these arguments for standards seem weak, especially in the longer term. It is, of course, possible that Instructions do, on balance, raise the quality of company accounts, even if less than is sometimes claimed. There appears to be little evidence of damage to investors in the absence of standards, nor of any reduction as a result of their appearance. In some respects standards may actually increase pressures on auditors. There is bound to be a substantial 'margin of error' in accounts in a complex world, and we should not exaggerate their possible precision. A classic American example of spurious accuracy is that of General Motors which as recently as 1975 reported its results to the nearest dollar. Standards cannot completely eliminate either fraud or error. If public expectations in this respect are too high, we should try to reduce them.

Arguments against Instructions include: restraining evolution; legitimising bad accounting and sometimes forbidding good accounting; stifling the exercise of independent judgement. It would be ironic if standards aiming to prevent short-termist company accounting turned out themselves to lead to serious long-term damage to accounting.

Having only a single source of accounting standards makes it vulnerable to capture; though at present there is wide circulation of exposure drafts before issuing accounting standards. Response levels to exposure drafts seem fairly low, perhaps because nobody expects the Accounting Standards Board to take much notice of anything but massive industry lobbying. Governments may be tempted to interfere if they dislike a proposed Instruction, as has happened in both the UK and the USA. Standards provide a channel for interference which would not otherwise exist.

Suggestions

Voluntary accounting standards ('Suggestions') seem to have several advantages over compulsory standards ('Instructions'). They leave the preparers and auditors of accounts free to exercise professional judgement; they would not inhibit further evolution, nor rule out any accounting methods providing a true and fair view. And Suggestions may be equally able to achieve two aims of Instructions: providing guidance on complex accounting issues; and helping to develop uniform language and layout in financial statements.

Suggestions need not aim to cover every possible case in detail, so they can be fairly short and simple. As an example, Appendix 3 (below, pp.70-72) sets out two possible 'Suggestions' – on Goodwill and Inflation Accounting. These are both knotty problems in accounting, yet the two Suggestions contain only about 500 words between them, say, two pages. ASB Financial Reporting Standards on these two topics, on present form, would almost certainly exceed 100 pages.

The idea of competing Suggestions has some appeal. The absence of a single source would reduce the temptation for an Instruction-issuing board to claim undue 'authority'. Indeed, it might be a good idea to issue Suggestions under the name of individual authors – mortals, so to speak – rather than some official board.

Sadly, however, in today's climate it seems unlikely that Suggestions would remain voluntary for long. People would accuse them of 'lacking teeth' (which, of course, they would, deliberately). It would probably not be long before some 'representative' body was busy 'co-ordinating' them. The feeble excuse that 'otherwise the government might step in' would no doubt be trotted out yet again; even though when government has directly interfered in accounting the result has usually been disastrous. I conclude that the choice is between compulsory accounting standards and none at all.

Costs

The direct costs of producing accounting standards are not huge.

The costs of observing them are probably much higher. And their longer-term indirect disadvantages may be still more serious.

Producing compulsory standards involves preparing discussion papers, then exposure drafts, then standards. (Not to mention a multi-part Statement of Principles, on which Financial Reporting Standards are supposed to be based, which is not yet complete.) But these production costs are not very large. In 1993/94 the Financial Reporting Council incurred operating costs of just under £¼ million, as did the Review Panel; while the Accounting Standards Board's costs were just over £¾ million. In contrast, total audit fees for UK companies total about £2,000 million a year.

Those imposing accounting standards do not bear most of the costs, and may not realise their extent. They may not even care. They may too readily assume that any benefit from standards automatically 'justifies' them. As with taxation, the costs of compliance exceed the direct costs manyfold. And, as with taxation, continual changes to the rules impose compliance costs too.

Some people think the ASB's Financial Reporting Standards since 1990 are far too detailed - nearly 400 pages of small print for seven standards. But the ASB claims that the lengthy explanation section in each standard is in response to consumer demand. (A rough split is: Essential: 20 per cent; Explanation: 24 per cent; Examples: 23 per cent; User Assistance: 33 per cent.) Voluntary guidelines, in contrast, can be short and general (see Appendix 3 for two examples).

Even if Suggestions were voluntary, there would probably be a stage similar to Exposure Drafts for standards. So the cost of producing Suggestions might not be much less than the costs of producing Instructions. Indeed, it might even be more in total if there were several 'competing' sources of Suggestions. On the other hand, presumably compliance costs could be a good deal less than for Instructions. And many of the longer-term disadvantages of Instructions would not exist at all with Suggestions.

Disclosure Standards, not Measurement Standards

An extreme contrast with the present system might be: 'Anything goes - if your auditors agree'. But there might be room for a compromise between them. Standards - compulsory ones - could emphasise the need for adequate disclosure but not try to prescribe the methods of measurement. This is hardly a new idea. As long ago as 1932 an AICPA Committee reported as follows to the New York Stock Exchange:

> 'In considering ways of improving the existing situation two alternatives suggest themselves. The first is the selection by competent authority out of the body of acceptable methods in vogue today of detailed sets of rules which would become binding on all corporations of a given class... The arguments against any attempt to apply this alternative to industrial corporations generally are, however, overwhelming.

> 'The more practicable alternative would be to leave every corporation free to choose its own methods of accounting within ... very broad limits ... but require disclosure of the methods employed and consistency in their application from year to year ... Within quite wide limits it is relatively unimportant to the investor what precise rules or conventions are adopted by a corporation in reporting its earnings if he knows what method is being followed and is assured that it is followed consistently from year to year.'[1]

This last point reflects the very sensible line often taken by the UK tax authorities. The effect would be to retain much of the accounting legislation in the Companies Act, which deals mainly with disclosure rather than with measurement. But scrapping standards on measurement would mean dropping sections 16 to 34 of Schedule 4 of the Companies Act 1985 dealing with accounting rules. (I would also be quite happy to scrap sections 6 to 8, the 12 pages dealing with formats of accounts.) It would also involve withdrawing 16 of the 25 accounting standards, leaving just nine standards dealing with disclosure: SSAPs 2, 3, 5, 17, 18, 25, and FRSs 1, 3, 4. The last three, in particular, could be much simplified. Elements of disclosure required by other standards could no doubt be restored if really necessary.

In the absence of standards, it might be useful to have a way of telling whether or not a particular accounting practice was 'generally acceptable' as capable of giving a true and fair view. Possibly some form of review by a 'jury' could help establish this. Such a jury, perhaps only half-a-dozen strong, could be drawn from lay people working in some area of accounting or business. They need not be 'politically correct'; indeed, Devlin says it is

---

[1]   Quoted in George O. May, *op. cit.*, Appendix to Ch.IV, p.76.

the so-called perversity of juries that justifies their existence.[2] For a start, such a jury might review the 'conceptual framework' on which standard-setters seem so keen.

On Balance

The volume of accounting Instructions is already high. If things go on like this, where will we be in 20 or 30 years' time? On balance I conclude we would be better off without any standards on accounting measurement. There could still be some disclosure requirements for listed companies, though probably less than now. There would still be pressure for listed companies to follow 'best practice'; and those that notably failed to do so would lose credit and reputation as a result. True, this approach excludes the Review Panel swooping to force offenders to 'correct' their accounts. But it leaves the way open for an independent profession to help accounting to evolve freely.

Nor would a 'retreat from standards' give the wrong signal. On the contrary, the kind of 'authority' claimed for accounting standards, especially those dealing with measurement, is unwise in intellectual and commercial matters. Members of the public (including journalists) should recognise the limits of company accounts. In particular, it is far easier to compare results within a single company over a period of years than between different companies. That may be unfortunate, but it is a fact. It is silly to aim for the impossible and then complain when you fall short.

In respect of accounting standards on measurement, I believe the cure is worse than the disease. The long-term effects, not merely short-term expediency, must be considered. We are ultimately concerned with an evolving process, not a static situation. National accounting bodies have been reluctant to accept 'standards' issued by other bodies; so why should individual accountants be any readier to have national standard-setters tell them what to do?

Governments should steel themselves not to interfere in matters which they do not understand and which they are ill-equipped to manage. Where professional bodies want to offer help to their members in coping with complex technical matters they should simply provide Technical Notes on a strictly 'take-it-or-leave-it' basis. Even Recommendations strive for – and eventually

---

[2]   Patrick Devlin, *The Judge*, Oxford University Press, 1979, p.131.

[62]

tend to get – more authority than is suitable in an independent profession.

Compulsory Instructions concerning measurement may seem tempting in the short term since they make it look as if someone is 'doing something'. But *laissez-faire* too has its benefits. Instructions have insidious effects in the longer term, which may not become fully apparent until it is too late to reverse the trend. Standards issuing orders on which accounting methods companies may and may not use can legitimise bad accounting and prohibit good accounting.

The present chairman of the Accounting Standards Board has written: 'In an ideal world, accounting standards would not be necessary.'[3] I agree. Even in the real world, accounting standards should be limited to disclosure requirements. They should not attempt to prescribe rules on measurement.

---

[3] David Tweedie and Geoffrey Whittington, *The Debate on Inflation Accounting*, Cambridge University Press, 1984, p.327.

APPENDIX I

UK ACCOUNTING STANDARDS as at 30 June 1995

SSAP		Topic	Issued	Revised	Pages
1		Associated Companies	January 1971	August 1974, April 1982	10
2		Accounting Policies	November 1971		6
3		Earnings Per Share	February 1972	August 1974, October 1992	15
4		Government Grants	April 1974	July 1990	9
5		Value Added Tax	April 1974		2
6	*	*Extraordinary Items*	April 1974	*Superseded 1992*	
7	*	*Current Purchasing Power*	May 1974	*Withdrawn 1978*	
8		Taxation (imputation system)	August 1974	December 1977	21
9		Stocks and Work in Progress	May 1975	September 1988	23
10	*	*Source and Application of Funds*	*July 1975*	*Superseded 1992*	
11	*	*Deferred Tax*	*August 1975*	*Superseded 1978*	
12		Depreciation	December 1977	November 1981, January 1987	9
13		Research and Development	December 1977	January 1989	11
14	*	*Group Accounts*	*September 1978*	*Superseded 1992*	
15	*	Deferred Tax	October 1978	May 1985, December 1992	16
16		*Current Cost Accounting*	*March 1980*	*Withdrawn 1986*	
17		Post Balance Sheet Events	August 1980		7
18		Contingencies	August 1980		5
19		Investment Properties	November 1981	*FRED9*	10
20		Foreign Currency Translation	April 1983		14
21		Leases & Hire Purchase Contracts	August 1984		11
22	*	Goodwill	December 1984	July 1989 *ED47* et al.	19
23		*Acquisitions and Mergers*	*April 1985*	*Superseded 1994*	
24		Pension Costs	May 1988		22
25		Segmental Reporting	June 1990		16
					226

* = subsequently superseded or withdrawn

[65]

APPENDIX I (continued)

FRS	Topic	Issued	Pages
1	Cash Flow Statements	September 1991	12 + 31 = 43
2	Subsidiary Undertakings	July 1992	22 + 24 = 46
3	Reporting Financial Performance	October 1992	13 + 25 = 38
4	Capital Instruments	December 1993	14 + 35 = 49
5	Reporting the Substance of Transactions	April 1994	13 + 74 = 87
6	Acquisitions and Mergers	September 1994	** 22 + 39 = 61
7	Fair Values on Acquisition	September 1994	** 14 + 46 = 60
			110 + 274 = 384

**FRS 6 and 7 in larger print than the others!

[66]

APPENDIX 2

CONFLICTS BETWEEN THE COMPANIES ACT 1985 AND UK ACCOUNTING STANDARDS

shown in order of the paragraph numbers in Schedule 4 of the Companies Act 1985

1.Para.3(2):   '... the following shall not be treated as assets in any company's balance sheet-... (c) costs of research.'

This contradicts SSAP 13 on Research and Development, para.16:

'Fixed assets may be acquired or constructed in order to provide facilities for research and/or development activities. The use of such fixed assets usually extends over a number of accounting periods and accordingly they should be capitalised and written off over their useful life.'

2.Para.3(7):   'Every profit and loss account of a company shall show separately ... (b) the aggregate amount of any dividends paid and proposed.'

With respect to dividends proposed but not yet declared, this does not square with FRS 5, para.4:

'Liabilities are defined as follows: Liabilities are an entity's obligations to transfer economic benefits as a result of past transactions or events.'

3.Para.12:   'The amount of any item shall be determined on a prudent basis, and in particular (a) only profits realised at the balance sheet date shall be included in the profit and loss account;'

Profits in respect of work-in-progress on long-term contracts are probably not 'realised' at the balance sheet date, yet SSAP 9 on Stocks and long-term contracts, para.29, requires such profit to be included where it can be assessed 'with reasonable certainty'.

The Companies Act prohibits the inclusion of profits on long-term contracts in the current asset amount shown for stocks and work-in-progress:

Para.22:   '... the amount to be included in respect of any current asset shall be its purchase price or production cost.'

Para.23: [or net realisable value if lower]

Hence awkward arrangements have been made in amending SSAP 9, to show as debtors any profit on work-in-progress on long-term contracts.

4.Para.12:   'The amount of any item shall be determined on a prudent basis, and in particular... (b) all liabilities and losses which have arisen or are likely to arise in respect of the financial year to which the accounts relate or a previous financial year shall be taken into account ...'

But SSAP 24 on Pension Costs, para.80, requires so-called past service costs to be spread out 'over the remaining service lives of current employees in the scheme'. This hardly seems to be 'a prudent basis'.

Indeed, para.82 explicitly restricts the application of a prudent basis of accounting, apparently in contradiction to the Companies Act:

'In strictly limited circumstances prudence may require that a material deficit be recognised over a period shorter than the expected remaining service lives of current employees in the scheme. Such circumstances are limited to those where a major event or transaction has occurred which has not been allowed for in the actuarial assumptions, is outside the normal scope of those assumptions and has necessitated the payment of significant additional contributions to the pension scheme.'

5.Para.14:   'In determining the aggregate amount of any item the amount of each individual asset or liability that falls to be taken into account shall be determined separately.'

This is inconsistent with SSAP 15 on Deferred Tax, paras. 25 and 26, which require use of the partial provision basis. Para.12 explains:

'Partial provision recognises that, if an enterprise is not expected to reduce the scale of its operations significantly, it will often have what amounts to a hard core of timing

[68]

differences so that the payment of some tax will be permanently deferred. On this basis, deferred tax has to be provided only where it is probable that tax will become payable as a result of the reversal of timing differences...'

SSAP 15 is thus clearly based on an *aggregate* approach to the tax liability, since the payment of tax will not be permanently deferred in respect of timing differences on particular individual assets. On an individual basis, which the Companies Act requires, either full provision or no provision is called for.

6. Para. 18:   'In the case of any fixed asset which has a limited useful economic life,... (b) where it is estimated that any such asset will have a residual value at the end of the period of its useful economic life, its purchase price or production cost less that estimated residual value...shall be reduced by provisions for depreciation calculated to write off that amount systematically over the period of the asset's useful economic life.'

This is inconsistent with SSAP 12 on Depreciation, para.12, which defines residual value as:

'the realisable value of the asset at the end of its useful economic life, based on prices prevailing at the date of acquisition or revaluation, where this has taken place.'

The Companies Act requires the *expected money amount* of the realisable value to be deducted from the purchase price or production cost in determining the amount of depreciation. It does not say anything about 'prices prevailing at the date of acquisition'; nor, in a system using money as the accounting unit of measurement, would this seem justifiable. Of course, the use of Constant Purchasing Power accounting would overcome this problem.

7. Para. 20(1):   '...an amount may only be included in a company's balance sheet in respect of development costs in special circumstances.'

SSAP 13 on Research and Development permits the capitalisation of development costs which meet certain 'stringent criteria' set out in paras. 10 to 12. It seems unlikely that meeting these criteria in SSAP 13 would be considered *automatically* to amount to the 'special circumstances' called for by the Companies Act.

APPENDIX 3A

SUGGESTION: ACCOUNTING FOR GOODWILL

1. Include purchased goodwill (including related intangible assets) at cost in the balance sheet, until fully written off; but not non-purchased ('internal') goodwill.

2. Amortise the cost of purchased goodwill through the profit and loss account, using the straight-line method or any more suitable accelerated method.

3. Amortise the cost of purchased goodwill to nil over its life, with a maximum of twenty years. Review each year to determine whether to reduce (never to extend) the life.

4. Review each year to assess whether the current value of purchased goodwill has fallen below the book amount. If so, write down at once through the profit and loss account. Do not revalue purchased goodwill upwards.

5. Write off any relevant unamortised goodwill through the profit and loss account against the disposal proceeds of any business segment.

6. Show the amount of goodwill resulting from each acquisition during the year.

7. Disclose details of purchased goodwill as for tangible fixed assets.

8. On the adoption of this Suggestion, reinstate in the balance sheet any purchased goodwill earlier deducted from reserves. Calculate the amounts as if this Suggestion had always been followed, and explain what they refer to.

APPENDIX 3B

SUGGESTION: ACCOUNTING FOR INFLATION

1. Show results for the period and the financial position at the end of the period in terms of constant purchasing power (CPP) units of a stated date.

2. Use the Retail Prices Index to translate unadjusted accounts.

3. Disclose separately the purchasing power loss or gain on monetary items.

4. If necessary redate corresponding amounts for previous periods into the same units of account as the current period.

5. Outline the method used to restate accounts originally prepared in foreign currencies.

6. Translate non-monetary items by restating them in proportion to the change in the purchasing power of money between the date of their acquisition or revaluation and the date of the CPP units. Translate monetary items only if the date of the CPP units differs from the balance sheet date.

7. After translation of non-monetary items, apply to current assets the test of 'lower of (translated) cost and (translated) net realisable value'. Similarly after translation of fixed assets, further provision may be necessary.

Definitions

8. Translation restates money amounts into terms of CPP units.

9. Unadjusted accounts are those prepared under established conventions, using money as the unit of account, including those in which some assets have been revalued.

10. Monetary items are assets, liabilities, or capital, the amounts

[71]

of which are fixed in terms of money regardless of changes in purchasing power.

11. Redating restates CPP units of one date into terms of CPP units of another date.

12. Non-monetary items are all items other than monetary items, except equity share capital and reserves.

13. Revaluation substitutes current values of non-monetary items for historical costs.

ACRONYMS

United Kingdom (UK)

AEI	Associated Electrical Industries
ASB	Accounting Standards Board
ASC	Accounting Standards Committee
ASSC	Accounting Standards Steering Committee
CBI	Confederation of British Industry
CCAB	Consultative Committee of Accountancy Bodies
DTI	Department of Trade and Industry
ED	Exposure Draft (for SSAP)
FRC	Financial Reporting Council
FRED	Financial Reporting Exposure Draft
FRS	Financial Reporting Standard
GEC	General Electric Company, The
HMSO	Her Majesty's Stationery Office
ICAEW	Institute of Chartered Accountants in England and Wales
ICAS	Institute of Chartered Accountants of Scotland
SSAP	Statement of Standard Accounting Practice
TUC	Trade Union Congress
UITF	Urgent Issues Task Force

United States (US)

AAA	American Accounting Association
AICPA	American Institute of Certified Public Accountants
APB	Accounting Principles Board
ARB	Accounting Research Bulletin
ARS	Accounting Research Study
ASR	Accounting Series Release
CAP	Committee on Accounting Procedure

FAS	Financial Accounting Standard
FASB	Financial Accounting Standards Board
FEI	Financial Executives Institute
FTC	Federal Trade Commission
GASB	Government Accounting Standards Board
SEC	Securities and Exchange Commission

Other

CCA	Current Cost Accounting
CPP	Constant Purchasing Power
EEC	European Economic Community
GAAP(UK)	Generally Accepted Accounting Practice
GAAP(US)	Generally Accepted Accounting Principles
IASC	International Accounting Standards Committee
IOSCO	International Organisation of Securities Commissions
NRV	Net Realisable Value
PE	Price/Earnings (ratio)

GLOSSARY

Current Cost Accounting. System of current value accounting which continues to use money as the unit of account (unlike CPP), but shows assets and expenses at current replacement cost (normally) instead of at historical cost.

Constant Purchasing Power (CPP) accounting. Method of inflation accounting which adjusts historical money costs of various dates by means of the retail prices index.

Deferred tax. Part of tax expense charged in accounts, not payable for some time due to timing differences between reported and taxable profits.

Goodwill. Excess of purchase price paid to acquire another company over the 'fair value' of the net separable assets acquired.

QUESTIONS FOR DISCUSSION

1. What are accounting standards trying to 'standardise'? Is this (a) desirable (b) possible?

2. What would happen if there were no 'accounting standards' of the sort we have today?

3. Is there a case for advisory voluntary standards ('Suggestions') rather than compulsory standards ('Instructions') as at present?

4. Who should be responsible for setting accounting standards? Why?

5. To what extent should Companies Act legislation set accounting standards, rather than the Accounting Standards Board?

6. Is it inevitable that the scope of accounting standards should expand over the years? Why? Where will the process end?

7. To what extent do you think accounting standards have achieved their aims?

8. Is it desirable for accounting standards in different countries to be 'harmonised'? Why? If so, which body should be responsible?

9. In which areas, if any, have the UK accounting standard-setting bodies failed in the last 25 years? What accounts for these failures?

10. If there is a 'gap' between what the public expects and what company accounts can deliver, is this because achievement is too low or because the public expects too much?

FURTHER READING

Beaver, William H., *Financial Reporting: An Accounting Revolution*, Englewood Cliffs, N.J.: Prentice-Hall, 2nd edn. 1986, especially Chapter 7.

Bloom, Robert and Elgers, Pieter T. {eds), *Issues in Accounting Policy*, New York: Harcourt Brace Jovanovich, 3rd edn. 1995, especially Part I (pp. 1-129).

Davies, Mike, Paterson, Ron and Wilson, Allister, *UK GAAP*, London; Ernst & Young and Macmillan, 4th edn. 1994, especially Chapters 1 and 2 (pp. 1-119).

Foster, George, *Financial Statement Analysis*, Englewood Cliffs, N.J.: Prentice-Hall, 2nd edn. 1986, especially Chapter 2.

Gore, Pelham, *The FASB Conceptual Framework Project 1973-1985*, Manchester University Press, 1992.

Naser, Kamel H. M., *Creative Financial Accounting*, Englewood Cliffs, N.J.: Prentice-Hall, 1993, especially Chapter 2.

Watts, Ross L., and Zimmerman, Jerold L., *Positive Accounting Theory*, Englewood Cliffs, N.J.: Prentice-Hall, 1986, especially Chapter 7.

Zeff, Stephen A., and Dharan, Bala G. (eds.), *Readings and Notes on Financial Accounting*, New York: McGraw Hill, 4th edn. 1994, especially Chapters 1 and 2 (pp. 1-130).

TAKING THE MEASURE OF POVERTY

RICHARD PRYKE

1. It is commonly believed that mass poverty has re-emerged, largely because that is the message conveyed by the DSS's *Households Below Average Income Statistics (HBAI)*.

2. But these statistics are open to serious objection. Alternative, more realistic statistics show much smaller numbers in poverty.

3. There are six major weaknesses in *HBAI*. They measure income by taking a 'snapshot', there is double-counting, they ignore the value of most goods and services provided free by the state, and the standardisation procedure for household size is dubious.

4. Particularly important, they disregard the benefits obtained from housing by owner-occupiers and those enjoying below-market rents, and they ignore the value of leisure.

5. When the DSS statistics are adjusted to provide a more appropriate measure of real income, a very different picture of poverty in Britain emerges.

6. Using the *HBAI* procedure for measuring income, between 10½ and 12 million people—around 20 per cent of the household population—were in poverty in 1988. But after adjustment to real income the number in poverty is only about 3½ million (6 per cent of the population).

7. The number in 'affluence' also declines after adjustment—from 5½ to 4 million (from 10 to 7½ per cent of the population). The wealthiest 10 per cent of the population receives less than five times as much as the poorest 10 per cent (compared with eight times before adjustment).

8. Existing *HBAI* figures are 'grossly misleading' and an '. . . economic nonsense [which] should not receive the stamp of state approval'.

9. The bulk of old-age pensioners are not poor, even if no value is placed on leisure, so there is '. . . little justification for a large or general increase in old-age pensions'.

10. In the long run, the present system of taxes and benefits seems 'unsustainable'. It is not equitable as between different income groups and involves perverse redistribution. Reform should concentrate on increasing the incentive to work rather than on reducing leisure.

ISBN 0-255 36371-0   Research Monograph 51   **£9.00**

THE INSTITUTE OF ECONOMIC AFFAIRS
2 Lord North Street, Westminster
London SW1P 3LB
Telephone: 0171-799 3745
Fax: 0171-799 2137

TAXES, BENEFITS AND FAMILY LIFE
HERMIONE PARKER

1. All income support programmes jeopardise work incentives. Yet it is important for the economy that work should be financially attractive and that extra effort and skill be rewarded.

2. Recent benefit changes and tax cuts have failed to improve work incentives for those on lower earnings.

3. A cumulative process of increasing disincentives is likely to increase the number of claimants, with the burden falling on diminishing numbers of taxpayers.

4. The tax and benefit systems also have an impact on family life. Recent changes mean that Britain is '...no longer a family-friendly country'.

5. The interaction of taxes and benefits now produces seven 'traps' – the unemployment/income support, invalidity, poverty, lone-parent, part-time, lack-of-skills, and savings traps.

6. Government under-estimates the problems of the present system and blames its victims. The issue is not so much 'scrounging': people are playing by the rules of a complex government-imposed game.

7. Spending on social security is out of control because governments which '...pay people for not working and for being "poor" end up with more people out of work and more "poor"'.

8. The present tax-benefit system should be replaced by a 'judicious combination of basic incomes (BIs: fixed amount tax credits which convert to cash for people without income to set against them) and income-tested benefits'.

9. An initial move to BIs could be made by converting personal tax allowances and child benefit into small transitional BIs – £20 a week for adults and £15·65 for children, which would cost the same as reducing the standard rate of income tax to 20%.

10. Britain's 'welfare' system is uneven between different categories of claimant and contains severe disincentives to effort. Fundamental reform is needed to remove perverse incentives which induce people to move themselves into categories where benefits are available.

ISBN 0-255 36370-2   Research Monograph 50   **£12.00**

THE INSTITUTE OF ECONOMIC AFFAIRS
2 Lord North Street, Westminster
London SW1P 3LB
Telephone: 0171 799 3745
Fax: 0171 799 2137